Women, Crime
and Criminology

Women, Crime and Criminology:
A Feminist Critique

Carol Smart

Department of Social Studies
Trent Polytechnic, Nottingham

Routledge & Kegan Paul
London, Henley and Boston

First published in 1977
by Routledge & Kegan Paul Ltd
39 Store Street,
London WC1E 7DD,
Broadway House,
Newtown Road,
Henley-on-Thames,
Oxon RG9 1EN and
9 Park Street,
Boston, Mass. 02108, USA
Filmset in 'Monophoto' Ehrhardt 11 on 12 pt by
Richard Clay (The Chaucer Press), Ltd, Bungay, Suffolk
and printed in Great Britain by
Fletcher & Son Ltd, Norwich
© Carol Smart 1977

ISBN 0 7100 8449 8

To Vera and Ernest

Contents

Tables

Tables

Acknowledgments

I have received help and support from many people during the writing of this book. In particular I want to thank Barry Smart for his unfailing intellectual and emotional support, and Mary McIntosh, Nigel Armistead, Ian Taylor and George Brown for their critical and constructive comments on various stages of my manuscript. Of course these individuals are in no way responsible for the completed work. I would also like to acknowledge the support I have received from members of the BSA Women's Caucus who gave me sufficient confidence to complete this book. Finally my thanks to Rene Shaw for typing my manuscript.

Introduction

This book began as a postgraduate dissertation which I wrote for a Master's degree in criminology. It was during this time as a postgraduate that I became aware of the overwhelming lack of interest in female criminality displayed by established criminologists and deviancy theorists. As I was interested in the topic of female criminality I began to do work in the area and soon came to realize that very few books on the subject were readily available. Even those that had been published were not to be found in libraries; in fact there was a considerable silence surrounding the whole area. I began searching for sources and found that quite a large number of articles had been written on female criminality and delinquency but these tended to be in medical journals or in American publications. Undeterred I collected material but it was not until I began to read it that I realized that the one thing most of the papers and books had in common was an entirely uncritical attitude towards sexual stereotypes of women and girls. From Lombroso and Ferrero (1895) to Cowie, Cowie and Slater (1968) and from W. I. Thomas (1967, originally published in 1923) to G. Konopka (1966) the same attitudes and presuppositions reappeared, confirming the biologically determined inferior status of women not only in conventional society but also in the 'world' of crime and delinquency.

The material that I uncovered presented mainly cultural stereotypes and anti-feminist ideology, the rare exceptions being papers by Heidensohn (1968), Klein (1973), Velimesis (1975) and a few others. Increasingly it became obvious to me that, as a first step at least, what was required was a feminist critique of existing studies of female criminality. The majority of these studies refer to women in terms of their biological impulses and hormonal balance or in terms of their domesticity, maternal instinct and passivity. I felt that such distorted views should not be left unchallenged and, although there is obviously a need for substantive empirical study of this subject, I was convinced that the existing ideological framework which supported the existing studies and theories had to be critically examined and revealed for what it was, namely fallacious and inadequate, before more empirical studies could cast any light on the phenomenon. I view this book therefore simply as a beginning, as an attempt to adopt a new direction towards the study of female criminality.

In writing such a book, documenting and criticizing existing studies, making a case for the necessity of further research on female criminality and delinquency, certain problems emerge. The first is that women and crime may come to be treated as a discrete area within criminology. That is it will receive a token lecture in a course on criminology along with such topics as mentally abnormal offenders or twin studies, while the main course will remain undisturbed, continuing to be concerned with the 'real' or 'important' issues, namely explaining male criminality and delinquency. Such a treatment of female criminality would ensure that the discipline of criminology could remain unmoved by any feminist critique. The second problem which arises is that of making female criminality into a visible social problem. I hesitate to add to a body of literature that might be used to identify or discover another 'problem', to create another 'moral panic'. It is not beyond the bounds of reason to imagine that if agents of social control and the mass communications media become sensitized to a new 'problem' their subsequent actions may well lead to the appearance of increases in the rates of crimes and an escalation in the reports of violent and criminal offences by women and of delinquency in girls. A comparable event was perhaps the 'appearance' of mugging in the early 1970s. Mugging, or mugging-type offences, were known previously in the UK but the adoption of a new label for an old offence created a situation in which it appeared that a new social 'problem' had emerged.

Female criminality may therefore become such a 'problem',

certainly public concern is already being expressed over the alleged increasing violence of juvenile girls. If an historical perspective on female criminality is adopted however then the topic of women and crime appears less like a new problem and more like one facet of human behaviour which has occurred in different forms at all historical moments. Moreover, a recognition of the need to bring the question of female criminality and delinquency into an open forum for discussion and debate is necessary in order that we may critically challenge the emerging moral panic over the relationship of women's emancipation to increasing participation by women in criminal activity.

The traditional studies of female criminality have remained unchallenged for too long, their ideologically informed, culturally specific explanations of the behaviour and nature of women, influencing both social research and policy, require critical re-appraisal and analysis. Critique is a prerequisite for the formulation of an alternative perspective.

Chapter 1

The nature of
female criminality

Our knowledge of the nature of female criminality is still in its infancy. In comparison with the massive documentation on all aspects of male delinquency and criminality, the amount of work carried out in the area of women and crime is extremely limited. The underdevelopment of this particular area of study seems to be in part a consequence of the pervasiveness of the belief in the relative insignificance of female criminality. Of course this belief in the insignificance of the actions of women, the assumption that women are inessential and invisible, is not peculiar to the domain of criminology or the sociology of deviance; on the contrary it is a feature of all aspects of sociology and academic thought. As Ann Oakley maintains,

The concealment of women runs right through sociology. It extends from the classification of subject-areas and the definition of concepts through the topics and methods of empirical research to the construction of models and theory generally (A. Oakley, 1974, p. 3).

Criminology as a subject discipline is therefore in no way unique in its consistently male-oriented bias, but as a policy-oriented social science it may be seen to have special implications for women which extend beyond the narrow confines of academia to the actual treatment of women in the courts and in penal institutions.[1]

A lack of interest in female offenders at the academic level is mirrored by a similar lack of interest by the Home Office and its policy-makers. With the exception of the rebuilding of Holloway

Prison, few changes have been made in the facilities available for female offenders who are institutionalized. The small number of penal establishments for women means that convicted offenders often have to be moved miles away from their home communities with obviously detrimental effects on sustaining familial and other relationships. Similarly, because of the lack of facilities for young girls who are deemed violent, we are experiencing the regrettable policy of placing juveniles into a prison like Holloway which still retains the characteristics of a fortress and a place for serious offenders.

It would be inaccurate however to argue that policy-oriented social sciences and policy-makers ignore the realm of criminal behaviour involving women simply because the offenders are women. We have, for example, no shortage of material on such areas as maternal deprivation or insanity and mental breakdown amongst women. It would seem therefore that women do merit research and study in certain circumstances, namely in the circumstances where women become definable as a social 'problem'. It seems likely therefore that the overwhelming neglect of female criminality is directly related to the low status of female offenders as a pressing social problem. In the past female criminality has not been thought to constitute a significant threat to the social order and even in the present, with the increases in the rate of offences committed by women, criminologists and policy-makers are slow to re-evaluate the notion that female offenders are little more than insignificant irritants to the smooth running of law and order.

Traditionally it has been argued that there has been little research or interest in the area of female criminality because statistically the numbers of female offenders have been so small and insignificant (cf. Heidensohn, 1968; Radzinowicz, 1937; Smith, 1974; Walker, 1973). Indeed official criminal statistics consistently provide us with the information that not only are female offenders fewer than male offenders but also that female offenders are, in almost all cases, a tiny minority. Consequently it has been maintained that there is not enough subject material to justify research. But statistical quantity alone is not sufficient to explain why female offenders are not yet treated as a social problem. It is necessary to consider also the types of crimes women commit which appear to be predominantly trivial offences involving very little monetary value or injury, or so-called sexual offences like prostitution. Moreover, with the exception of prostitutes, it appears that most female offenders who appear in court are first offenders who are deterred from further crime more readily than male offenders (Walker, 1973). Women and girl offenders, in contrast to male offenders, therefore present less of an irritation to the police, the courts and the penal system and consequently there has been little official requirement or support for studies of female criminality. As a result of this lack of official concern, orthodox, control-oriented criminology, which has been involved in serving the needs of administrators and policy-makers, has virtually ignored the existence of female offenders. The very nature of criminology as a discipline, its traditionally narrow concerns with only those topics officially designated as social problems and its attempts to find the causes and solutions to such problems, is responsible for the sorry state of current knowledge and work on female criminality. Moreover those studies which do exist, with very few exceptions, have failed to develop beyond the most un-critical and ideologically-informed works produced during the 1940s and 50s. As Ward states in the Report to the US National Commission on Crimes of Violence, 'Our knowledge of the character and causes of female criminality is at the same stage of development that characterized our knowledge of male criminality some thirty or more years ago' (Ward et al., 1969, p. 847).

An important consequence of this lack of development has been the total neglect of any critical analysis of the common-sense perceptions of female criminality informing classical (Lombroso and Ferrero, 1895; Pollak, 1961) and contemporary studies (Konopka, 1969; Cowie et al., 1968). Hence many unexplicated, culturally specific assumptions about the 'true nature' of women which are inherent in common-sense understandings have come to constitute the basis of criminologists' attempts to comprehend 'scientifically' the nature of female crime. It is not surprising there-fore that many myths, from the theological belief in the funda-mental evil and weakness of Woman to the paternalistic belief in Woman's frailty and gentleness, still prevail in accounts of female criminality.

3

The lack of interest in female criminality which is displayed by orthodox criminology has also had the effect of rendering it insignificant to more contemporary schools of thought within the discipline. There appears to have been no need to counter the conservative tradition with a more liberal perspective, nor indeed to replace the liberal tradition with a radical or critical analysis largely because of the insignificance of female criminality in the 'old' criminology. Virtually by default therefore inadequate and ideologically informed studies have become the main or major sources of reference in this area, no substantial body of criticism being readily available to reveal their limitations. In contrast, in the case of studies of male criminality a certain progression may be traced from the classical school of Beccaria, to the emergence of positivism which upholds a belief in biological or psychological determinism, to the subcultural and interactionist theorists and finally to those works displaying a Marxist influence. With the study of female criminality this development has largely been arrested at the positivist stage with the result that our present understanding of female deviance is based predominantly upon biological or psychological drives and urges which are deemed to be peculiar to the female constitution or psyche. The exception to this pattern of arrested development within criminology is the interactionist study of prostitution; the supposed sexual deviation of prostitutes being well suited to the focus of deviancy theory in the 1960s, preoccupied as it primarily was with victimless crimes and 'vices'. The main thrust of theories of female criminality has however remained in the hands of the positivists with the result that theories relating to female criminality, even more than those concerned with male criminality, support and justify the prevailing methods of treatment and the ideology of social control adhered to by the administrators of legal and penal policy. This relationship between positivism and social control has been well documented, although its specific influence in relation to female offenders has been overlooked. For example Taylor, Walton and Young state,

For the politician and the planner, positivism provides a model of human nature which, in its consensual aspects, allows the world 'as it is' to remain unquestioned and, in its determinist notion of human action, offers the possibility of rational planning and control (Taylor *et al.*, 1973, p. 35).

In a situation in which even the classical concepts of self-determination have always been denied to women (their mental and moral capacities being likened to children and lunatics) the advent of positivism has merely served to confirm common-sense perceptions about women in general and female offenders in particular —namely that they are prey to their biological and psychic constitution.

It is certain that many myths prevail in studies of female offenders and yet before these can be dispelled it is essential to discuss the nature of female criminality as it appears to theorists who have attempted to provide accounts and explanations. In order to understand the basis of many theories of female criminality it is necessary to know which crimes women apparently engage in and to what extent they are, or appear to be, involved in criminal careers. Furthermore, as the assumptions and opinions inherent in studies of female criminality are generally dependent upon, or derived from, some kind of statistical evidence, usually extracted from official criminal statistics, the statistical picture of female crime acquires additional significance in any analysis of the theories and practice of female criminality.

The statistical basis of the common-sense perception
of female criminality

I have already noted that the most well-documented feature of female criminality derived from available statistical information is the relatively few numbers of women who engage in what is legally defined as crime. However, the proportion of women who engage in crime varies quite considerably according to the nature of the offence. For example, in the case of shoplifting official statistics show that, with the exception of the figures for 1974, the numbers of female shoplifters usually exceed the numbers of males. Where an offence like the theft of a motor vehicle is concerned, however, the numbers of female offenders are a very small percentage of the numbers of male. (For example, in 1973 a mere 737 women were convicted of this offence compared with a total of 31,222 men found guilty.) In general the numbers of women offenders rarely exceed men but some of the offences included in the official statistics actually exclude the members of one sex by legal definition, thereby creating some wholly 'female' or 'male' offences. I will refer to this category of offences by the term 'sex-specific' crimes and will differentiate them from those offences which may be committed by either sex but which in practice are more common to one sex than the other. These latter offences I will refer to as 'sex-related' crimes.

Sex-specific offences

There are very few sex-specific offences in the English legal system as the law is, in principle, held to be equally applicable to all regardless of sex, race, class and other distinctions. One exception to this is infanticide which is an offence that only women can commit. In effect infanticide is the legal recognition of post-natal depression in women. It is an offence which can only be committed when the balance of a woman's mind is disturbed 'by reason of her not having fully recovered from the effects of giving birth to the child' (Smith and Hogan, 1973).[2] Infanticide constitutes only a very small category however; a more significant example of a sex-specific offence is prostitution. The English law recognizes that both men and women can be prostitutes and since the Sexual Offences Act of 1967 it has been an offence for a man or a woman to live off the earnings of either a male or female prostitute. But although male prostitutes are recognized, the category of 'offence by prostitute' in the Official Statistics relates only to women; men are not charged with this, which in fact refers mainly to soliciting. A superficial reading of the statistics therefore gives the impression that prostitutes are inevitably female, a not accidental consequence of the attitude of administrators who feel justified in allowing soliciting to remain an offence for women while the solicitation of women by men (kerb crawling) remains a lawful activity. Unlike infanticide there is no complex biological factor which can be said justifiably to exclude one sex from the legal category termed prostitution; on the contrary the

failure to include offences committed by males which are prosti-
tutive in character exemplifies a purely legal, moral and social
decision. When male 'prostitution' does appear in the statistics it
is included with non-prostitutive homosexual offences like 'importuning by males' or 'indecency between males' and so statistically
it becomes impossible to distinguish between male prostitutes and
male homosexuals.[3]

The situation with regard to prostitution is similar in the USA
where the legal definition of prostitution, which varies from state
to state, is often described as 'the practice of a female offering
her body to an indiscriminate intercourse with men, usually for
hire' (Hoffman-Bustamante, 1973). This in effect excludes males
from the possibility of being charged with a prostitution offence.[4]
The practice of excluding one sex from legal sanction or of applying
different legal categories according to sex, whilst the action in
question is comparable, is highly suspect and open to the charge of
sexual discrimination. In many ways it may be compared with
racist laws which make it illegal for certain races (e.g. Blacks and
Coloureds) to engage in certain actions which are perfectly legal
for other races (e.g. Whites). However, while the injustice of the
latter is apparent it has not yet been similarly established where
sexual differences are concerned.

The question of sex-specific offences (whether exclusively male
or female) raises the question of whether the criminologist should
be content to work within the legal framework which produces the
official criminal statistics. Most studies of prostitution for example
have adopted the statistical picture of prostitution as a virtually
exclusively female offence. Furthermore such studies have tended
to accept that prostitution, or at least soliciting, should be a
criminal offence while at the same time accepting that the clients
of prostitutes should not be prosecuted (Davis, 1971; Pollak, 1961).
In so doing there has been a tacit and occasionally an overt legitimation of aspects of the legal code which are based on double
standards of acceptable behaviour for men and women. As Garfinkel, Lefcourt and Schulder (1971) maintain, 'The laws are a
formal codification of attitudes towards women that permeate our
culture', and consequently to work uncritically within the framework of the law is to accept the past and current common-sense

perceptions of the nature of women (and men) which inform the law. The failure to treat the law itself as a topic for analysis has meant that criminologists have remained unaware that the position of women *vis-à-vis* the law may be significantly different from that of other groups in society. In other words, it has not been recognized that criminal laws, like civil laws, are man-made in the interests of men in accordance with a paternalistic attitude towards women. Hence although sometimes in practice and even in principle women are at a disadvantage in law[5] criminologists, content to work within the parameters of the legal definition of crime, have remained unaware of, and consequently uninterested in, existing discriminatory circumstances and forms of treatment.

Sex-related offences

Sex-related offences are those crimes which may be committed by either sex but which in practice appear to be committed more by one sex than the other. Because of the small numbers of female offenders in general it is not surprising that most offences are termed 'masculine', that is they are more commonly committed by males. There are exceptions to this however. For example, prostitution may be classified as a sex-related offence (as well as a sex-specific offence) because it is legally recognized in the UK that men can be prostitutes even though male prostitutes are hard to detect in the official statistics. Only in legal codes where male prostitutes are not recognized at all would prostitution be by definition fully sex-specific. Shoplifting is also an offence which, according to official statistics, is usually committed more frequently by women than men, and in spite of the large numbers of men who are convicted of shoplifting, it remains an offence which is thought of as a predominantly female activity (see Table 1.1). This is in spite of the fact that proportionately more men than women have been convicted of shoplifting since 1972. The assumption that shoplifting is mainly a female activity is undoubtedly related to the fact that the numbers of women officially recorded as involved in shoplifting far exceed the numbers of women involved in any other type of crime, which makes shop-

Table 1.1   *A comparison of male and female offenders found guilty of shoplifting as a proportion of total male and female populations in England and Wales*

Year	Number of persons* found guilty of shoplifting		Population of † England and Wales in thousands		Persons found guilty of shoplifting per 100,000 of population	
	Male	*Female*	*Male*	*Female*	*Male*	*Female*
1969	17,051	20,833	23,561·8	24,978·5	72	83
1970	18,853	21,739	23,626·3	25,053·8	80	87
1971	21,181	23,070	23,737·2	25,117·2	89	92
1972	22,406	23,513	23,840·7	25,197·6	94	93
1973	22,564	22,738	23,915·8	25,258·8	94	90
1974	28,636	28,019	23,941·0	25,254·1	120	111

* Source: *Home Office Criminal Statistics for England and Wales*, 1969 to 1974, Table IV(a) Indictable Offences, all Courts, all ages.
† Source: *Population Trends*, Autumn 1975, Table 2, p. 21, HMSO, London.

lifting quite unique in terms of female offences. Male and female shoplifters, although they do not appear to vary greatly in terms of their statistical significance, are apparently quite diverse in terms of the items they steal. According to Gibbens and Prince (1962) who studied shoplifting in 1959 and 1960, women steal mostly food, usually of little value, and clothes, while men tend to steal books and objects other than food or clothes, frequently of considerable value. A similar pattern emerges in the USA where a large percentage of larceny charges involving women are for shoplifting where the items stolen are of little value (Hoffman-Bustamante, 1973).

The involvement of women and girls in shoplifting and their choice of stolen goods would seem to be closely related to the gender role of women in industrial societies like the UK and the USA. Women are predominantly shoppers for household items and food and the techniques of shoplifting, unlike the techniques which might be required for other offences such as car theft or burglary, are as

9

available to them as to all shoppers. The tremendous increase in large self-service supermarkets which display goods in such a way as to tempt the shopper to buy are also clearly instrumental in the increase in shoplifting in general and food thefts in particular (Gibbens and Prince, 1962). The theft of clothes is also clearly linked to the feminine role. This is particularly evident where pressure is placed on women to be well dressed and fashionable while the prices of clothes are restrictive and women's average earnings low. Shoplifting can therefore be seen as an extension of the feminine role, it is 'role-expressive' both in method and in its object, unlike other forms of deviance which appear to contradict the traditional, stereotyped, female sex role.

A comparison between typical male and female sex-related offences is shown in Table 1.2(a) and (b) where the statistics clearly indicate the types of offences most usually committed by men and women in the UK and the USA.

Table 1.2(a)   *Some examples of the statistical basis of sex-related offences in the UK*

Type of offence	Number of persons found guilty	Male offenders as a % of all those found guilty	Female offenders as a % of all those found guilty
Offence by prostitute and related offences*	3,781	18·5	81·5
Shoplifting	45,302	49·8	50·2
All larceny	180,875	80·7	19·3
Car theft	31,959	97·7	2·3
All burglary	54,362	96·7	3·3

Source: *Home Office Criminal Statistics for England and Wales*, 1973, Table IV(a) Indictable Offences, all Courts.

* Offences related to prostitution are 'aiding offence by prostitute', 'male or female living on earnings of male or female prostitute', 'brothel keeping' and 'importuning by a male'.

Table 1.2(b)   *Some examples of the statistical basis of sex-related offences in the USA*

Type of offence	Number of persons found guilty	Male offenders as a % of all those found guilty	Female offenders as a % of all those found guilty
Prostitution/ Commercial vice	49,344	20·7	79·3
Larceny	616,099	72·1	27·9
Auto theft	127,341	94·9	5·1
Burglary	285,418	95·3	4·7

Source: *FBI Uniform Crime Reports*, 1970, reprinted in Hoffman-Bustamante (1973), pp. 133–4.

Sex-related offences are not peculiar to adults however and although the statistics in Table 1.2 include offences by juveniles there are special categories of 'offences' which are applicable only to adolescents which require special attention. These 'offences', which are defined as non-criminal in the UK, usually relate to truancy from school, being beyond the control of parents or being in moral danger. There are similar categories of juvenile offences in the USA, for example 'curfew' or 'runaway', which have the same connotations as being in moral danger or being beyond control. The statistics indicate that, of these 'offences', those most frequently involving girls are, in the UK, being in moral danger, and in the USA, running away (see Table 1.3). This is significant because both of these categories of offences have connotations of sexual promiscuity. Consequently the statistics present a picture in which female juvenile delinquency appears to be mainly sexual while male juvenile delinquency is apparently non-sexual but more aggressive and assertive. Certainly studies of female juvenile delinquents have accepted this premise and have proceeded to attempt an explanation of the promiscuity of adolescent girls (Richardson, 1969; Cowie, Cowie and Slater, 1968; Gibbens, 1957). Usually promiscuity in both girls and women is, like shoplifting, described as 'role-expressive' behaviour. In other words a concern with sex as a means to a desired goal is seen as fitting to the typical

Table 1.3(a)   *Sex-related 'offences' involving juveniles in care proceedings in the UK, 1973*

Proceedings brought under Children & Young Persons Act, 1969	Total number of proceedings, ages 10–17		Percentage of offenders	
	Male	*Female*	*Male*	*Female*
S1(2)(a) development neglected, ill-treatment, etc.	761	757	51	49
S1(2)(c) exposed to moral danger	48	377	12·4	87·6
S1(2)(d) beyond parental control	309	472	39·5	60·5
S1(2)(e) not receiving full-time education	1,121	977	53·3	46·7
S1(2)(f) guilty of an offence, excl. homicide	19	11	63	37

Source: *Home Office Criminal Statistics for England and Wales*, 1973, Table V(a) Care Proceedings (Non-criminal proceedings at Magistrates' Courts).

Table 1.3(b)   *Sex-related 'offences' involving juveniles in the USA, 1970*

Type of offence	Number of persons found guilty	Percentage of offenders	
		Male	*Female*
Curfew	105,548	78·8	21·2
Runaway	179,073	48·4	51·6

Source: *FBI, Crime in the United States*, 1970, printed in Hoffman-Bustamante (1973), p. 134.

feminine role. The bargaining of sexual favours for the appropriate goal, namely marriage, is taken to be the inevitable destiny of all girls. As Davis maintains, 'As a scarce means, sexual access can be deliberately withheld or made available by an attractive person. Sexual desirability is thus an asset that can be traded for economic and social advantage' (Davis, 1971, p. 317). It is only when sex is used to bargain for what is termed as an inappropriate goal (i.e. prostitution) or when a girl fails to bargain at all or bargains while she is 'too young' that deviancy occurs. If it is argued that deviancy or criminality are reflections of the major concerns of our life-world, then male criminality, which is largely concerned with the acquisition of goods or wealth either by theft, fraud or violent means, reflects both the major concerns of the breadwinner who must support a family and the desires of younger men to have prestige in their peer groups. But because the life-world of women is said to revolve around securing a mate or living vicariously through their men, the argument follows that the only field of deviance 'appropriate' to a woman's role, besides shoplifting, is sexual deviance.

Shoplifting, prostitution in adults and promiscuity and 'un-governability' in adolescents are the only 'offences' that the statistics reveal to be predominantly 'female offences'. That is, it is only in these forms of deviance or criminality that the numbers of female offenders exceed male offenders. There are, of course, other crimes in which women engage to a significant extent and which are closely related to the female sex-role. These include handling stolen goods, social security offences, petty forgery and even murder. Even though relatively few women appear to commit these sorts of offences, it is still possible to see such crimes as related to the typical female role, if only in terms of the techniques adopted for the implementation of the offence or the choice of victim.

Other offences committed by women

The other categories of offences involving women to a fairly significant degree are shown in Table 1.4. Those most obviously related to the female sex-role concern offences against children and infants. For example offences like cruelty to a child, abandoning a child under two and even child stealing are clearly more likely to be committed by women who bear most of the responsibility for child care. The stress of looking after children, the stigma of illegitimate birth and the desire to have a child are almost entirely peculiar to women in our culture. Similarly with procuring illegal abortions, the burden of restricted access to legal medical abortions falls mainly on women who must ultimately give birth to unwanted

Table 1.4 *Additional indictable and non-indictable offences according to the sex of the offender—all Courts, all ages*

Offence	1959		1969		1974	
	Male	Female	Male	Female	Male	Female
Indictable						
Murder	35	—	74	1	108	4
Attempted murder	20	2	39	7	45	7
Other wounding*	7,099	283	17,879	939	28,234	2,084
Theft by employee	7,199	1,304	8,815	1,389	9,969	1,855
Theft from a machine	3,681	467	7,262	1,551	3,734	1,001
Handling stolen goods	5,505	565	17,483	1,895	18,433	2,590
Forging & uttering	1,676	948	2,048	911	2,535	1,046
Cruelty to a child	4	—	12	12	15	24
Child stealing	N/A	N/A	5	8	7	10
Procuring illegal abortion	5	12	29	23	4	7
Non-indictable						
Cruelty to a child	340	301	156	187	76	95
Drunkenness, simple	29,988	2,595	37,184	3,133	46,551	3,412
Drunkenness with aggravation	28,140	1,812	34,919	1,785	44,801	3,093
Social Security offence	538	164	1,873	703	2,982	1,503
Other motoring offences†	530,879	28,493	850,187	60,437	1,023,688	79,803

Source: *Home Office Criminal Statistics for England and Wales*, 1969 and 1974, Tables IV(a) Indictable Offences and Tables IV(b) Non-indictable Offences.

* Other wounding refers to wounding other than endangering life.

† Other motoring offences refer to offences excluding driving or in charge of a vehicle while unfit, reckless or dangerous driving and driving while disqualified.

children without this service. Of course the number of illegal abortions reported in the official statistics is most likely to be an understatement primarily because those most affected by the offence are unlikely to report it to the police. Consequently the proportion of men and women actively engaged in procuring illegal abortions is hard to estimate although it is reasonable to assume that because pregnancy concerns mainly women in our culture, more women than men are involved in procuring illegal abortions.[6]

Table 1.4 also includes the statistics on theft by an employee, theft from an automatic machine or meter and handling stolen goods. Although women do not constitute a very large proportion of these offenders their participation is significant in so far as the personal relationships and illegitimate opportunity structures involved in committing these offences represent an extension of the 'normal' feminine gender role rather than deviation from it. For example, in the case of offences involving the handling of stolen goods the recipient of the goods is likely to be a 'passive' associate who has not participated in the original theft or burglary. This 'passivity' is in keeping with the woman's role especially where stolen goods are hidden or used in the home. Furthermore it is frequently the case that women will conceal stolen goods for those with whom they have some kind of personal relationship, for example husbands, lovers or sons, and they therefore become implicated in criminal behaviour through 'family' loyalty. In the case of theft from a machine the personal relationship element, present in other types of offences, is entirely missing and such a theft is a purely impersonal act of a very petty nature, involving no victim. Stealing from a machine requires no great skill, strength or aggression so consequently it is in keeping with the culturally ascribed characteristics of the female role. Similarly theft from an employer does not necessarily require much planning or skill. In the types of jobs where women are frequently employed, such as domestic work or as shop assistants, there are opportunities for thefts which cannot be easily detected because of the size of the organizations involved, or high staff turnover or even because of shoplifting by customers. Of course most occupations give some opportunities for dishonesty and it is likely that as women become a larger part of the workforce more of them will be involved in offences of this nature.

None of these types of offences requires particularly 'masculine' attributes. Strength and force are unnecessary and there is only a low level of skill or expertise required. The women involved have not required training in violence, using weapons or tools, or in specialized tasks like safe breaking. On the contrary the skills required can be learnt in everyday experience, and socialization into a delinquent subculture or a sophisticated criminal organization is entirely unnecessary. Even forgery does not always require particular skills beyond the level of literacy which men and women are equally likely to acquire. Hoffman-Bustamante maintains that forgery is consistent with the female sex-role; she states,

we can again propose that as in the case of larceny, the high proportion of women [forgers] is due to the fact that the crime fits well into the everyday round of activities in which women engage, especially their role of buying most family necessities and paying the family bills (Hoffman-Bustamante, 1973, p. 126).

A similar case can be argued for social security offences especially where legislation is particularly punitive towards unsupported women who have been deserted, widowed or have never married. In such a situation a woman may attempt to claim more financial aid than she is legally entitled to, especially if she is 'cohabiting' with a man. This is because legally it is assumed that a man who is living with a woman is supporting her financially whether or not he really is and regardless of whether he is actually in employment. Women are therefore likely to be involved in social security offences quite frequently, especially where cohabitation is involved. In this case their involvement in crime is related mainly to the state's re-inforcement of their economically dependent position in society and to their role of provider for children and the home.

Violent offences on the other hand do not appear to be easily reconciled with the traditional conceptualization of feminine behaviour. Murder and other violent acts against the person appear to be the complete antithesis of the gentle, retiring, caring role of the female sex. Indeed in the UK very few women appear to be involved in such offences and for this reason 'violent' women, such as female terrorists, are often dismissed as pathological exceptions to nature's laws. Studies of violence, in particular homicide, in the USA do suggest however that although violence enacted by women is relatively infrequent, the choice of victim and the *modus operandi* of the offence are still in keeping with the 'feminine' stereotype. For example, Wolfgang's (1958) major analysis of homicide reveals that the victims of the female murderers he studied were over-whelmingly individuals who had a 'family' relationship with the offender (51·9 per cent) or who were 'paramours' (20·9 per cent). Women therefore appeared to murder their husbands, lovers and other relatives while the men in the study more frequently killed close friends and strangers. Women offenders, according to Wolf-gang, also tended to use less physical strength in committing murder, for example they were far less likely to beat a victim to death or to use excessive violence, such as multiple stab wounds, on their victims. Women used knives or household implements in over a third of the cases and tended to kill their victims in the kitchen or within their own homes. This finding fits well with the socialization processes experienced by most women for while they become used to handling kitchen knives they have rarely had the opportunity to learn how to fight or use their physical strength effectively. Wolfgang also suggested that the place of the killing and the weapon used, as well as the fact that the crime was often unpremeditated, implied that many homicides by women were victim precipitated. In other words, he argued that the eventual victim was often the original aggressor and that the women often killed in self-defence or in anger. Significantly a more recent study of women imprisoned for homicide by Ward (1969) indicates that 42 per cent of their victims were unable to defend themselves. That is they were either ill, drunk, off-guard, asleep or infirm. These conclusions concerning the way in which women dispatch their victims are of course a reflection of the disparity between the physical strength of men and women. Most women are unlikely to succeed in killing a fully conscious, fit and able-bodied man, although it is of course not impossible. Ward's findings do not necessarily refute Wolfgang's concept of victim precipitation, however. On the contrary, the discovery that a large percentage of the victims in Ward's study were unable to defend themselves may indicate only that the women waited for an opportune moment to commit a murder which had been motivated by the victim at some earlier stage. Women therefore seem to commit homicides most frequently within the context of the family, often in self-defence or in a victim precipitated interaction, and in spite of the fact that violent behaviour appears to be relatively less common amongst women than men homicide by women can be understood in terms of their traditional role within the home.

Conceptual problems inherent in the statistical analysis of female criminality

Our understanding of female criminality is largely based on the picture presented to us by official statistics and empirical research. Consequently those studies which have uncritically accepted the available statistical data have treated as given the belief that fewer women than men are involved in criminal behaviour and that the type of offence most frequently committed by women and girls (with the notable exception of shoplifting) is sexual in nature. Additionally because there appear to be so few female offenders they are conceived in these studies to be abnormal in both a biological and a psychological sense and their criminality is explained in terms of physiological and psychological factors which are held to be peculiar to the female sex. Thus, whereas men are considered to turn to crime for economic or social reasons or through poor socialization, women are believed to become criminals because of their menstrual cycle or menopausal symptoms (cf. Dalton, 1961; Pollak, 1961). Or then again women are considered to become prostitutes because of unresolved oedipal conflicts and maternal deprivation (cf. Greenwald, 1958) while men using prostitutes are not treated as sexually deviant, recourse to a prostitute being treated as merely expressions of a 'normal' male sex drive (cf. Davis, 1971; Wilson, 1974). Such conclusions are an inevitable consequence of the adoption of the legal definition of crime and an uncritical acceptance of official criminal statistics because it is these sources which indicate to us that female offenders are 'unusual' or that prostitution is a predominantly or even a wholly female activity.

It is significant that few studies of female criminality have been critical of official statistics as a resource. It is after all well known that the numbers of offences cleared up by the police are a small percentage of those offences which are reported and an even smaller percentage of those which never come to light. The existence of this hidden figure is inevitably ignored however when official statistics are used to make statements about female criminality. One major exception to this generally accepted practice is the work of Otto Pollak (1961) which concentrates to a considerable extent on what he terms the 'masked' nature of female criminality. Basically Pollak argues that women are more able than men to disguise the extent of their criminality because of their position in society. He maintains that because of the privatized existence of most women their crimes are unlikely to come to light. For example, as mothers and child-minders they have abundant opportunity to engage in child-molestation or neglect and yet this is hard to detect because of the privacy of the home and what Pollak terms the revered status of Mother. Similarly he argues that it is easy for women to murder and remain undetected because, being the preparers of meals, they are able to poison their victims and hence kill discreetly and avoid detection. To a certain extent the arguments proposed by Pollak are valid. There is little reason to doubt that women engage in more crime than is revealed in the official statistics although his apparent belief in poisoning-at-will is somewhat difficult to accept. What is even harder to accept however is Pollak's contention that male criminality is not similarly masked. He maintains that the amount of crime committed by men reported in the statistics is a true reflection of the 'actual' amount of male criminality. He quite overlooks that, unlike most women, men may operate in both a public and a private sphere such that they too may have the protection of the privacy of their homes in which to commit certain offences (i.e. assaulting wives and children). His contention that women are as criminal, or even more criminal, than men is therefore purely speculative although his work is of some significance if only in the observation that women may commit offences more often than is generally assumed.

Since the publication of Pollak's work there have been several attempts to measure 'hidden' crime in order to correct the deficiencies of official statistics. In particular Wise (1967) has attempted to disprove the assertion that girls commit predominantly sexual offences by comparing self-reported offences to the official statistics. The results of her research indicate that boys and girls participate equally in sex and alcohol offences (50·1 per cent of boys and 49·9 per cent of girls commited sexual 'offences' and

50·8 per cent of boys and 49·2 per cent of girls committed alcohol 'offences'). With other offences there was not equal participation, the boys offending more than the girls, but the difference between the sexes was not as great as implied by the official statistics. The question that is raised by these results is how to account for the discrepancy between the self-report figures and official statistics, in particular where sexual 'offences' are concerned, for, as it has already been observed, the statistics give the impression that female delinquency is largely sexual, unlike male delinquency. Before attempting to deal with this question, however, it should be noted that self-report studies are not without faults and possible distortions. Morris (1965) has revealed in a study of attitudes towards delinquency that girls show more shame over delinquent acts, as measured by their unwillingness even to admit to offences known to the police. The boys on the other hand were inclined to boast, as measured by questions relating to the degree of pride felt over a delinquent act. The results of hidden delinquency studies therefore cannot compensate for the way in which the subject of the study defines the situation of an interview and reacts or responds accordingly.[7]

Returning to the question posed by the results of Wise's study, it is important to consider the way in which the official statistics, which are themselves the final product of interpretative processes within the criminal process, may be influenced by the operation of a double-standard of morality. Two studies of juvenile offences in the USA supply significant information on this question and on the treatment of delinquent girls by the police and judicial process. The first study by Terry (1970) indicates that because of the sexual nature of the offences frequently committed by girls there is a tendency for them to be treated more severely than boys whose offences are rarely defined as sexually promiscuous or deviant. Terry's data, which are based on police statistics for a heavily industrialized mid-west city during the years 1958 to 1962, indicate that a disproportionately large number of girl offenders, compared to boy offenders, were referred to social and welfare agencies by the police. This type of referral is judged by Terry to be a fairly severe type of treatment and he argues that it is the most usual method of disposal for cases of a sexual nature or incorrigibility. Consequently he maintains that the reason why a disproportionately large percentage of girls receives this type of referral is that the majority of offences by girls are either sexual or incorrigibility cases. Clearly if proportionately more girls than boys commit a certain type of offence which almost automatically carries a referral which is defined as a fairly severe form of treatment then proportionately more girls than boys will receive that type of treatment. Terry points out that although girls committed only 17·9 per cent of all the offences in the police records, they were responsible for nearly half of the sex offences and incorrigibility cases, and this, he argues, accounts for why girls appear to be treated more severely than boys by the police. Similarly, at the level of the juvenile court, Terry indicates that girls are more severely treated than boys yet again. He finds that girls are proportionately far more likely to be institutionalized than boys even though the girls have less extensive records of delinquency. Once again Terry implies that the reason for this type of severity is because of the sexual implications of many of the offences committed by the girls and because the judiciary finds it more shocking to have a girl in court than a boy. The consequence of such attitudes towards female offenders where they commit sexual offences is that such girls are likely to be overrepresented both within institutions and in police and welfare agency statistics, creating the appearance that girls predominantly commit sexual offences which are serious enough to result in institutionalized punishment. Such data are however more likely to display the attitudes of welfare agencies and the judiciary than to reflect the differential behaviour of delinquent girls and boys.

One major failing of Terry's study is that he accepts as given that proportionately more girls than boys commit sexual offences. At no stage does he attempt to consider why girls constitute such a large proportion of sexual offenders while they constitute such a small percentage of offenders overall, nor does he question why so-called sexual offences such as sexual intercourse while under age should automatically lead to relatively severe treatment by the police and courts. A study by Chesney-Lind (1973) attempts to explain these phenomena by studying the 'rate-producing processes' of the juvenile court in Honolulu. Basically Chesney-Lind argues that the juvenile court in the USA (and I would maintain in the UK also) reflects the double-standard of morality present in the wider society. Consequently any sexual behaviour by a girl who is either under age or unmarried is treated as a very serious misdemeanour even though it offends morality rather than criminal statute. The same behaviour on the part of a boy is treated as appropriate and 'natural', however, requiring adults to 'turn a blind eye' rather than to be morally outraged. But Chesney-Lind goes further than this for she does not argue that juvenile courts merely concentrate on sexual (mis)behaviour by girls, she also maintains that they actively sexualize offences committed by girls. This process of sexualization is achieved by creating offences which are either explicitly sexual or which include the possibility of sexual infraction such as running away or incorrigibility. It is further achieved by administering physical examinations to suspects in order to discover whether or not they have been sexually active. This procedure then serves to increase the possible number of offences with which a suspect may be charged or to modify the original charge. In other words a simple charge of larceny may be modified to include incorrigibility if the girl offender is suspected of being sexually 'promiscuous'. Chesney-Lind states,

The sexualization of offenses, or the casting of specific law violations into the broader categories of incorrigibility, running away or sex delinquency, is suggested then not only by the court's skewed offense distribution but also by the court's routine use of pre-trial physical examinations and lengthy detention in the processing of females brought before the court (Chesney-Lind, 1973, p. 57).

Although no specific studies have been carried out in the UK to discover whether female juvenile offences are sexualized in the same way as Chesney-Lind suggests occurs in the USA there are some data available which indicate certain similarities. For example, Richardson (1969), in her study of girls in approved schools, points out that a large majority of girls who were technically non-offenders were admitted for being in moral danger or in need of care and protection and further that over one third of the sample of five hundred girls studied were institutionalized after only one court appearance. She adds, by way of a qualification, that although such a large proportion were institutionalized when they had officially committed no criminal offence most of them were 'known' to be petty thieves or to have committed an offence at some stage. Now leaving aside the question of how it is possible to 'know' that a number of girls, who are institutionalized on the basis of their sexual deviancy, are also guilty of other offences in circumstances where they have not been officially accused or found guilty of such crimes, it is highly significant that these girls should be placed in care on the basis of their sexual (mis)behaviour rather than being tried for their criminal activities. Whereas it is most unusual for an adolescent without a previous criminal record to be placed in an institution for committing a criminal offence such as larceny or even violence, there appears to be in the case of a girl, also without a criminal record, a considerable likelihood that she will be placed in an institution if she is thought to be sexually promiscuous. It would seem therefore that in the UK there is more than a possibility that juvenile offences by girls are sexualized, that is to say certain non-sexual offences are overlooked in favour of proceedings based on sexual (mis)behaviour. This process means in effect that girls receive most severe treatment because sexual deviance in girls is generally felt to warrant institutionalization while comparable behaviour in boys is rarely considered deviant at all. An important consequence of this process is that in both the USA and the UK official statistics show a high rate of sexual delinquency for girls and further severe punishment for many female 'offenders'. Traditionally this has been superficially interpreted as indicating that girls are more sexually deviant and, because they are treated severely, it has been assumed their offences are of a serious nature. Only when the practices of the juvenile and magistrates' courts are examined however is it revealed that such interpretations are unwarranted and that a sexual bias in court proceedings actually influences the picture of female juvenile delinquency presented in the official statistics.

Official statistics represent a limited and problematical basis from which to commence an analysis of female criminality and delinquency. In addition to the problems inherent in their use which I have outlined above there are other drawbacks which are especially relevant to the study of female offenders which have not been sufficiently stressed in other critiques of official statistics (e.g. Wiles, 1970). In particular the grounds for assuming that the apprehended population of women offenders is in any way representative of all women offenders are unfounded. It is by no means the case that female offenders (any more than male offenders) who are caught or reported and the types of offences they are convicted of are representative of offenders or offences as a whole. With shoplifting for example it is well known that different shops at different times adopt widely different policies about prosecuting shoplifters. This means that our knowledge of shoplifters is entirely contingent upon the discretion of store detectives, shop managers and company policies. With other offences like forgery, fraud and theft the likelihood of arrest is directly related to the ability and skill of the offender. It is likely therefore that the least able and the most petty offenders form a disproportionate number of those apprehended. Hoffman-Bustamante (1973) points out that the types of illegitimate opportunities open to women are precisely the sort of offences that the police in the USA are more likely to investigate, i.e. 'con' games or welfare frauds. In contrast the opportunities open to men also include more discreet forms of white-collar crime such as false advertising, product defects and occupationally oriented frauds which are far less likely to be detected. Traditionally these 'safe' forms of white-collar crime have not been open to women because of sexual discrimination in employment and the small numbers of women in positions of authority and influence, hence women have been restricted to the more risky, petty offences.

The question of the illegitimate opportunity structures traditionally open to women raises the question of whether changes in women's social and economic roles are leading to higher rates of criminality. Certainly the official statistics give the impression that women are engaging more frequently in more varied forms of crime (see Tables 1.4 and 1.5). Since 1959 increases have been recorded in offences like burglary, robbery, theft and handling stolen goods, drunkenness and fraud. In contrast common assault and offences by prostitutes appear to be on the decline. Long range comparisons of this nature are, however, very unreliable

Table 1.5(a) *Numbers of females found guilty of selected indictable offences (all Courts)*

Offence	1959	1969	1973	1974
(Malicious) wounding	299	939	1,939	2,084
Burglary in a dwelling	394	898	963	1,067
Going equipped for stealing	4	33	38	30
Robbery	45	138	184	147
Theft from the person	101	93	195	226
Theft by an employee	1,313	1,389	1,755	1,855
Theft from a machine	471	1,551	1,247	1,001
Handling stolen goods	612	1,895	2,056	2,590
Other fraud	162	1,465	1,981	2,405

Table 1.5(b) *Numbers of females found guilty of selected non-indictable offences (Magistrates' Courts)*

Offence	1959	1969	1973	1974
Common assault	1,462	1,152	709	497
Drunkenness, simple	2,595	3,133	3,435	3,412
Social Security Act (formerly National Assistance)	164	703	1,329	1,503
Drug offence	N/A	N/A	1,571	1,202
Offences by prostitutes	12,264	2,318	2,976	2,964

Source: *Home Office Statistics for England and Wales*, 1959, 1969, 1973 and 1974, Tables IV(a) Indictable Offences and IV(b) Non-indictable Offences.

largely because of the numerable changes in the criminal law which alter categories of offences and police policies.[8] It is problematical whether women are committing more offences or whether they are merely being apprehended, charged and convicted more frequently. In addition as the increase in female criminality does not appear to be proportionately greater overall than the increase in male offences (cf. Heidensohn, 1968) it is difficult to assess whether or not female criminality is increasing at a more alarming rate than male criminality. There is however an impression created by changes in the official statistics, that female criminality and delinquency are becoming more serious and more of a threat to the social order. Whether this is the result of changes in the 'real' behaviour of women and girls or whether it merely reflects a growing awareness on the part of theorists and policy-makers that women also play an active part in committing crimes in our society is hard to determine. As Heidensohn remarks in her analysis of the reasons behind the lack of interest in female criminality,

One need not go as far as to argue that the high rates of sociological interest in a problem area produce appropriately high 'problem situation' responses; but one might well be forgiven for wondering whether the deviance of women is a non-problem both to the social scientist and to society in general, because so little effort has been devoted to studying it (Heidensohn, 1968, p. 162).

An interest in the role of women in all spheres of social life has been growing since women's groups and movements have begun once again to question the low social status of women and to demand changes in opportunities available to, and discrimination suffered by, women in virtually all strata of society. It is inevitable, therefore, that some criminologists will attempt to place the responsibility for the apparent changes in female criminality and delinquency on the Women's Movement rather than seeing both as an outcome of changing social and economic conditions (cf. Hart, 1975; Ward et al., 1969; Konopka, 1966). But whatever the 'causes' of the apparent increase in female criminality and the very real increase in interest by policy-makers and professional pathologists, offences by women and girls are becoming a new 'social problem'.

Chapter 2

Classical studies of female criminality

The most significant early studies of female criminality are the works of Lombroso and Ferrero (1895), Thomas (1967, originally published 1923) and Pollak (1961, originally 1950). They may be termed classical studies not only because of the stage of development within criminology in which they were written, but also because they are virtually 'pioneer' studies in the area of women and crime. Unlike other pioneer studies which have been surpassed and have become redundant though, these accounts of female criminality are still, in some form, exerting an influence on contemporary understandings of female crime. Their influence lingers on largely because of the lack of interest in this area shown by criminologists, a disinterest which is evident in the paucity of critical studies of female criminality. An additional reason for the continuing 'relevance' of these particular works is the compatibility of their ideological stance with the prevailing interests of professional pathologists and agents of social control. This common stance, which unites these classical theorists even though their accounts of female criminality vary widely, is based upon a particular (mis)conception of the innate character and nature of women, which is in turn founded upon a biological determinist position. This emphasis on the determined nature of human behaviour is not peculiar to the discipline of criminology, nor to the study of women, but it is particularly pertinent to the study of female criminality because of the widely-held and popular belief in the non-cognitive, physiological basis of criminal actions by women.

The genesis of this particular mode of thought is found at the end of the nineteenth century in the work of Lombroso, who has been called the founding father of the biological-positivist school in criminology. Lombroso's brand of positivism removed the study of crime and criminals away from legal experts and social scientists and made it the domain of human biologists, medical doctors and subsequently psychiatrists and psychologists. To a large extent the study of male criminality has been retrieved by the more sociologically oriented studies produced by 'liberal' and 'radical' sociologists, but female criminality has in contrast remained predominantly within the sphere of interest and control of medical and psychological professions. Lombroso's form of positivism was based on two premises. First, on a belief in the superiority and neutrality of scientific work, and second, on a belief in the determined character of human nature. The first premise assumes that the methodology appropriate to the natural sciences is fitting also for the study of human, social relationships and the socio-economic order. Consequently attempts were made (and still are made) to reduce human behaviour to quantitative rather than qualitative statements, to compare the actions of human beings to those of lower primates and other animals and to discover the 'laws' that dominate human action comparable to the laws that are believed to operate in the physical and material world. At the time Lombroso was writing the most influential natural science was biology and the evolutionary theories of Darwin were accepted wholeheartedly into the study of human behaviour. Biological criteria were therefore treated as the epitome of 'scientific' work with the result that Lombroso and some of his successors concentrated on biological and physiological factors to the detriment of social criteria. The adoption of this particular natural-science method also had the consequence of affirming the supposed neutrality of the scientists and their work. Just as the natural scientists were assumed to be neutral in their choice and methods of study so the early social scientists believed themselves to be free from cultural influence, prejudice and personal involvement. The fallacy of this belief will be discussed below; it suffices to say here that the work of Lombroso and his successors is firmly located in its cultural context, failing to rise above the common-sense perceptions, myths and ideologies in general currency at their respective stages in history.

The pervasiveness of the belief in the scientificity of positivist methodology has produced a lasting rift between the so-called keepers of knowledge and the lay person. The professional or the scientist was (and is) held to have the solutions to human problems but this knowledge was (and still is) not shared, made communicable or available in order that people may become more self-determining. On the contrary the knowledge produced was (and still remains) privatized and geared to increasing the control of the professional over the lives of others. This development is linked closely to the second major premise of positivist criminology, namely the belief in the determinism of human nature. Adoption of determinism, whether biological or psychological, serves the purpose of ideologically displacing the possibility of self-determination with a scientific legitimation of either existing material constraints and external controls or the introduction of new social control technologies. It is therefore the complete antithesis of an emancipatory project, a project oriented towards self-consciousness and a realization of the possibilities for radically changing material conditions; instead it is oriented towards the provision of information and techniques relevant to the possibility of exercising more efficient control over any behaviour deviating from a predetermined set of norms. Thus social deviants or criminals who do not act according to predefined normative standards are diagnosed as pathological, requiring 'treatment' in order to produce conformity. Within this paradigm deviant individuals are not considered to be social critics, rebels or even members of a counter culture, rather they are treated as biological anomalies or as psychologically 'sick' individuals. Their actions are not interpreted as having particular social significance, as being possibly rational responses, and in consequence such individuals are perceived as aberrations who must be 'cured' or removed from society. In this way the positivist school maintains that there is a clear distinction between criminals or deviants and 'normal' members of society, these differences being assessed by such criteria as 'signs of degeneration' (e.g. Lombroso and Ferrero, 1895) or scores on an extraversion–introversion scale (e.g. Eysenck, 1970).

Such is the legacy of positivism created by Lombroso and its influence will be demonstrated throughout this book. But there have been other influences on students of female criminality such that although other classical writers and their successors largely share in the positivistic heritage additional influences may be perceived. In particular the work of W. I. Thomas (1967) is indicative of the growth of liberalism in criminology and the perpetuation of the seemingly benevolent 'treatment' perspective in opposition to more punitive policies. This perspective, which has been wholeheartedly adopted by welfare and social work agencies, has had considerable effect on the treatment of adolescent offenders, resulting in particular in an extensive legal interference in the lives of young adults (cf. Platt, 1969). Pollak's work (1961), on the other hand, displays not so much liberal benevolence as a traditional theological belief in the basic evil of women; in this respect he is close to Lombroso. Surprisingly, despite the apparent contradictions between the 'theological' premise at the heart of Pollak's work and the more liberal perspectives exemplified by Thomas, both themes manage to survive in contemporary theories of female criminality. These contradictory themes are able to co-exist only because the presuppositions about the inherent nature of women which inform these perspectives are never examined. The assumption that women are evil and malicious and gentle and caring is part of our cultural heritage; it is quite possible to adhere to the belief as long as it is never questioned or made fully explicit. Consequently such (mis)conceptions and prejudices have remained implicit and unaddressed because their validity is taken for granted and their self-evident nature is shared with all members of our culture. These contradictory assumptions are not only commonly shared in all sections of society however as, in practice, they are also referred to for confirmation of 'scientific' postulations on the causes of female criminality. For example, in one instance the naturally cunning or evil woman is invoked to explain child neglect or murder while in another instance the exploited, misled, unprotected woman-child is invoked to explain prostitution. Some contemporary criminologists, like Cowie, Cowie and Slater (1968) or Richardson (1969), may be seen to move from one invoked image to another without any apparent discomfort, and remain sublimely confident that their culturally-loaded common-sense observations are neutral in the extreme, carrying no 'biased' pre-suppositions. But before proceeding to analyse the full impact of the classical theorists on contemporary understandings of female criminality, it is essential to consider the works of Lombroso and Ferrero, Thomas and Pollak in some detail in order to demonstrate their ideological similarities and their major weaknesses.

Lombroso and Ferrero

Lombroso and Ferrero's study of women and crime, *The Female Offender* (1895), is fundamentally based on the now discredited concepts of atavism and social Darwinism. The concept of atavism refers to the belief that all anti-social or criminal elements in society are in fact biological throwbacks from an earlier evolutionary stage in human development. In his early works Lombroso firmly maintained that deviants are less highly evolved than 'normal' law-abiding citizens although he was forced to abandon this position to some extent in his later works because of excessive criticism. Social Darwinism on the other hand refers to the belief that individuals or groups can develop necessary physical or psychological charac-teristics to enable them to function more efficiently in their pre-determined roles. Thus, for example, Lombroso argued that prostitutes evolve in a way that makes them unusually attractive when young while in contrast murderesses or violent women evolve an unusual strength.

In the fashion of the earlier works on male criminals Lombroso and Ferrero studied pictures of female offenders, measured craniums and counted the moles and tattoos of imprisoned women in order to find consistent signs of degeneration or atavism. Significantly, although they found some signs of so-called degeneration like misshapen skulls or very thick black hair, the female offenders in their study did not fit well into the theory of atavism. Very few of this somewhat unrepresentative sample were of the 'true' criminal type, better known as 'born' criminals. This was because in order to be a complete criminal type Lombroso and Ferrero estimated that four or more signs of degeneration must be present in the offender's physiology and only a tiny minority of female offenders and a slightly larger proportion of prostitutes measured up to this criterion. Rather than abandoning the theory of atavism however, they used the concept of biological determinism to explain why 'true' criminals are rarely found among the female population. It is this aspect of Lombroso and Ferrero's work that is of special interest for, although the crude theory of atavism is now recognized as an amusing and slightly unfortunate episode in the development of criminology, modified versions of their biological account of the infrequency of female criminality still survive.

Lombroso and Ferrero argued that women offenders reveal fewer signs of degeneration simply because they have evolved less than men. Having developed less far from their origins, they argued that women could also degenerate less far and so, being as all women are relatively 'primitive', the criminals amongst them would not be highly visible and would be less degenerate than their male counterparts. They accounted for the less evolved nature of women in terms of the lives women *naturally* lead. In other words they saw women as less active than men, leading a sedentary existence because of their biologically determined role of child-minders. Men, on the other hand, were considered to be the sole providers for the family, and were therefore depicted as leading active and challenging lives which resulted in their greater evolutionary advance over women. Moreover Lombroso and Ferrero maintained that conservatism in women has led them to be more law-abiding than men. This conservatism was not thought to be culturally induced however; on the contrary Lombroso and Ferrero argued that it has organic origins. They stated,

Compilers of public statutes have also noted the conservative tendency of women in all questions of social order; a conservatism of which the primary cause is to be sought in the immobility of the ovule compared with the zoosperm[1] (Lombroso and Ferrero, 1895, p. 109).

Consequently Lombroso and Ferrero perceived women to be congenitally less inclined to crime than men and so the true criminal type and even the occasional criminal were considered rare amongst women. But in spite of their rarity Lombroso maintained that the born female criminal makes up for what she lacks in relative numbers by the excessive vileness and cruelty of her crimes.[2] The born female criminal was perceived to have all the criminal qualities of the male plus all the worst characteristics of women, namely cunning, spite and deceitfulness. Moreover such women were thought to represent not only an 'unnatural' combination of both sexes, they were also believed to be abnormal in their lack of any maternal instinct. For Lombroso and Ferrero this 'deficiency' was the ultimate proof of the abnormality and degeneration of criminal women. It was the clearest sign that these women were genetically more male than female. For example they argued,

This want of maternal feeling becomes comprehensible when we reflect on the one hand upon the union of masculine qualities which prevent the female criminal from being more than half a woman, and on the other, upon that love of dissipation in her which is necessarily antagonistic to the constant sacrifices demanded of a mother. Her maternal sense is weak because psychologically and anthropologically she belongs more to the male than to the female sex (Lombroso and Ferrero, 1895, p. 153).

Such confusions between sex and gender, and the perception of masculinity and maleness in female offenders, is a recurrent theme in most studies of female criminality. The logic of Lombroso and Ferrero's argument is based on a belief that the true, biologically determined nature of women is antithetical to crime. For men on the other hand, criminality is a more common feature of their natural characteristics. Hence if a woman is a true criminal type she is not only an abnormal woman she is biologically like a man. This myth assumes however that because there is a biological and chromosomal basis to sexual differentiation (i.e. male/female) there is also an equally immutable biological basis for gender differentiation (i.e. masculine/feminine). Now there are two major fallacies in this belief. First, the biological basis of sexual differentiation is not immutable and may in fact be considered fluid. Evidence to support this is supplied by the incidence of the birth of individuals without specific sexual characteristics and by the case of later development of secondary sexual characteristics at puberty which are of the opposite sex to the primary sexual organs. In both of these cases sex can be seen as indeterminate or as changeable, the two sexes do not have a polar relationship but are shown to be opposite ends of a continuum with the possibility of overlap and combined sexual characteristics. Moreover the availability of hormone treatment and surgery which allows transference from one sex to another makes the artificial alteration of sexual characteristics a constant possibility (cf. Garfinkel, 1967).[3] Second, while sex is a biological term, gender is a social, cultural and psychological term and this proposition has been supported by several anthropological studies (i.e. Mead, 1967; Oakley, 1972). For instance Oakley states,

It is true that every society uses biological sex as a criterion for the ascription of gender, but beyond that simple starting point, no two cultures would agree completely on what distinguishes one gender from the other (Oakley, 1972, p. 158).

And again later,

The biological predisposition to a male or female gender identity (if such a condition exists) may be decisively and ineradicably overriden by cultural learning (Oakley, 1972, p. 170).

Hence it can be seen that although certain types of behaviour are labelled 'masculine' it is both a social and a relative concept which is not biologically fixed and which can be appropriated by either sex without there being any corresponding biological anomaly. However, in the work of Lombroso and his successors (cf. Cowie, Cowie and Slater, 1968) the women who adopt typically 'masculine' forms of behaviour become labelled 'masculine' themselves and this has connotations of 'maleness' which can, it is maintained, be traced to a biological base. Consequently, 'true' female criminals are biologically abnormal, because first they are rare and second they are not fully female. In effect this myth produces a situation in which female offenders are doubly damned for not only are they legally sanctioned for their offences, they are socially condemned for being biologically or sexually abnormal. As Lombroso and Ferrero stated, 'As a double exception, the criminal woman is consequently a monster' (Lombroso and Ferrero, 1895, p. 152). Lombroso and Ferrero consistently failed to appreciate that because of the apparent rarity of serious or violent offences by women when such cases did occur they would seem all the more shocking. That is to say when a comparable crime is (or was) committed by both a man and a woman social reaction against the woman would be much more severe because different standards are (or were) applied to measure the behaviour of the different sexes. Female offenders are therefore monstrous not because of their innate qualities but because they are socially defined as such.

The majority of Lombroso and Ferrero's female criminals were not true criminal types but only what they termed occasional criminals. They accounted for their existence by making reference to a combination of environmental and biological factors, but the biological factors were the key elements in their analysis. For example although they admitted that modern department stores present a temptation to steal they argued that women succumb easily because they are naturally less honest than men. Unlike the born criminal who has the same moral development as a child, the occasional criminal was perceived to have adequate 'moral equipment' and to possess sufficient chastity and maternal love. She was however held to be generally weak-willed and easily led into crime, the performance of which was frequently abysmal, leading to instant arrest. Her inadequacy in this field was held to be a reflection of the inferiority of women as a whole and her role in the commission of an offence, generally as an accomplice or someone else's tool, was seen as fitting to her 'natural' role.

The concept of woman's 'natural' role or her 'true nature' is absolutely fundamental to Lombroso and Ferrero's work. They arrived at their assessment of what that 'true nature' might be through uncritical, experiential perceptions of middle-class women in Europe during the nineteenth century. Consequently they believed that the inferior social position of women, their inactive lives, their apparent lack of genius and socially desirable skills, their concerns with trivia and luxury as well as their petty rivalries, were true reflections of the nature of Woman. Lombroso and Ferrero totally overlooked historical and anthropological evidence of the activities and social position of other women in other periods and societies. They assumed that what they witnessed in their historical era was the only possible arrangement of the social order and therefore the 'natural' one. In turn they 'proved' that this was the 'natural' order of things by providing evidence of the way in which the 'normal' women in their society behaved. In other words they proclaimed, in common with other determinists, that 'things are as they are because they are natural and they are natural because that is the way things are'. The drawback with this tautology, besides the fact it tells us nothing, is that it reaffirms Lombroso and Ferrero's failure to go beyond the apparent reality of everyday life to question how that reality was achieved. This failure to attempt to transcend the apparent natural character of the social order resulted in them studying female criminality in total isolation from the context in which it occurred. They merely selected one institution in society and studied it in isolation from all other social, economic, cultural and historical phenomena. Having wrenched the study of crime from its social context and origins in an attempt to discover a single biological causal factor, Lombroso and Ferrero were unable to recognize, let alone account for, the influence of such factors as socio-economic status, the creation of laws, the role of agencies of social control, increasing urbanization and the development of capitalism on criminal activity. Such factors as these were for Lombroso and Ferrero merely the 'triggering' incidents which enabled an inherent pathology within the individual to be revealed. Consequently, although they referred to these so-called environmental factors, they were not given the same status as biological and physiological criteria which were the cornerstones of biological positivism.

Lombroso and Ferrero's work on female criminality has served to create an ideological framework in which later, more contemporary studies have developed. Variations on the belief in biological determinism, both of crime and the nature of women, on sexist beliefs in the inferiority of women and an implicit support of double-standards of morality, along with the failure to take account of the socio-economic, political and legal context in which 'crime' occurs, all appear in later works on female criminality. Thus although Lombroso and Ferrero's theories of criminality are now accepted as intellectually inadequate and morally distasteful their influence remains. As Matza succinctly puts it,

Lombroso said bodily constitution and to his close or careful readers muttered something about social conditions; nowadays, we say social conditions and to our close or careful readers mutter something about organic conditions (Matza, 1969, p. 90).

W. I. Thomas

The works of Thomas are indicative of the development of a liberal tradition in criminology. This liberalism rests upon the individualization of social 'problems' and ultimately on methods of individual treatment or 'cure'. It carries over from Lombroso's work a belief that criminality or deviance is a pathology, but that it is a socially induced pathology rather than a biological abnormality. This liberalism requires that individual offenders be treated as undersocialized, as not fully adapted to the social values of society which represent their interests, and ultimately as being 'sick' rather than inherently evil or rationally opposed to the dominant values of society. The liberal tradition therefore displays a benevolent aspect and it became very popular with social reformers who espoused humanitarian values and supported moderate social change which did not threaten the economic and political structure of society. Liberalism was particularly well received by welfare agencies and social workers dealing with children and adolescents who were either troublesome or who had 'criminal tendencies'. Children, rather than adults, were perceived to fit into the liberal ideology with considerable ease because child status was synonymous with a lack of responsibility for action. It was easier to regard children as in need of help rather than punishment, because of their perceived lack of moral development. Social workers also held out greater hope of rehabilitation for children as their 'criminal' characters had not been so irretrievably formed. A concern for what children were becoming rather than what they had done was also engendered by this perspective and consequently liberal reformers became preoccupied with the hypothetical future moral well-being of the child rather than the specific legally defined misdemeanour. In this way a rationale was supplied for imposing moral standards on children which were (and are) not applicable to adults. Intervention into a child's life, which would not be tolerated by an adult, was justified on the grounds that potential delinquents should be reformed before they became morally degenerate. Signs of potential delinquency included such behaviour as lying, sexual activity and mere precociousness; and being indicators of 'criminal tendencies' they were held to merit some form of treatment or institutionalization.

Thomas's work spans a transitional period. His later work, *The Unadjusted Girl* (1967), which was first published in 1923, shows the full impact of the new liberal ideology and displays a highly functionalist perspective (the basis of most American sociology and criminology of that period). In contrast his earlier work, *Sex and Society* (1907), was more influenced by a Lombrosian biological/physiological approach. For example, in the latter when analysing sexual differences he utilized the concepts of the 'katabolic' male and the 'anabolic' female. Katabolic referred to the destruction of energy, a process which was believed to result in creativity while anabolic meant the storing of energy and resulted in passivity. Thomas therefore employed supposed physiological differences between the sexes as a resource in accounting for variations in the social behaviour of men and women. In this particular respect his account is very close to Lombroso and Ferrero's reference to the hyperactivity of the male's sperm in comparison to the inactivity of the female's ovaries. Both Thomas and Lombroso and Ferrero assumed that physical differences could explain why only men became politicians, great artists or intellectual giants. They ignored both the fact that women were denied access to such achievements in their own respective cultures (for example through the privatized nature of child-care or preventive legislation) and overlooked the fact that women were extremely creative and active within the fields in which they were able to operate. Such selective representation of the nature and behaviour of women was not merely a reflection of male hegemony and paternalism but also of class bias because the life-styles and life-chances of working-class women were overlooked in favour of the middle-class norm. This is a particularly surprising omission in the case of Thomas as his major concern was the plight of immigrant, often peasant, women in the USA, who not only worked outside the home but often had to rear children single-handed. The work of both these theorists contains therefore not only elements of sexism (that is, the attribution of socially undesirable or inferior characteristics to one sex which are based on a confusion between socio-culturally and historically produced features and supposedly inherent or 'natural' characteristics of that sex) but also a class bias which interprets all social behaviour in terms of a middle-class value system.

Thomas's (1967) later work on delinquent girls is based less on a simple biological determinist perspective and incorporates the familiar nature-nurture debate, in which nature is viewed as supportive of environmental factors. His analysis of human social behaviour is based on a concept of 'wishes' which are derived from biological instincts but which may be channelled towards appropriate goals through socialization. 'Wishes' are therefore not freely[4] chosen, they impel the person to act while cultural norms provide the means and ends which satisfy the basic desires or instincts. The basic wishes that Thomas defined as fundamental to human nature were the desire for new experience, for security, for response and for recognition. These wishes were said to correspond to features of the nervous system which were expressed as the biological instincts of anger, fear, love and the will to gain power or status respectively. However, the biological instincts in men and women were not perceived to be equal in quantity or quality, as Thomas believed that women had more varieties of love in their nervous systems. Consequently a woman's desire for response was thought to be more intense than a man's. In particular Thomas referred to the so-called maternal instinct which women are assumed to feel in response not only to their own children but also to sick or helpless adults (particularly men). He argued that it was this additional and intense need to give and feel love that leads women into crime, particularly sexual offences like prostitution. The prostitute, he argued, is merely looking for the love and tenderness which all women need, but the means by which she seeks satisfaction are not socially approved. The apparent logic in Thomas's analysis of the basis of female criminality has several defects however. First, there is no consensus of opinion over whether or not there is such a thing as a maternal 'instinct' inherent in the nervous system of women. This is not to deny that maternal 'feelings' exist but merely to indicate that there is an important distinction to be drawn between feelings and instincts. Instincts are held to be fundamental features of our physiology and psyche, they are essentially beyond our rational control and if they are found to be lacking it can be presumed that this is evidence of an abnormality. Thus it is frequently maintained that the mother who has no love for her child is 'unnatural'. Feelings, on the other hand, are more easily controlled and because there is such an abundance of different feelings to be experienced which are not linked to a biological imperative it is not considered a sign of abnormality if feelings vary from person to person. Consequently if maternal feelings exist, rather than instincts as Thomas maintained, then it is possible to argue that paternal feelings in men are the equivalent to maternal feelings in women. This would then allow for the varieties and intensities of love and affection to be found in both sexes to be equal as opposed to Thomas's conception of the unequal distribution of affective needs and responses. Culturally of course we have come to assume that men do not feel emotion or affection in the same way as women. Men who cry, who show tenderness in public, who embrace each other are not 'real' men within our cultural understanding of that term. Male children are punished for being effeminate while girls are encouraged to be soft, gentle and caring. Thomas was therefore merely reflecting his own cultural beliefs about the capacity for love in men and women by resorting to concepts of biological instincts which are fixed, virtually finite and immutable. He perceived a certain reality in the relationships of men, women and children and assumed that it was the 'natural' order of things. Hence he sought for a 'natural' or biological explanation, using environmental factors only to explain the different modes by which inherent instincts are expressed.

The role of natural or biological factors in Thomas's work did not however submerge the significance of the concept of the subjective definition of the situation, which was such a major aspect of his analysis of social phenomena. It was Thomas's theory that the objective reality of a situation was less important to the behaviour and beliefs of the individual than his or her subjective definition of that reality. Thus if an individual felt deprived, whether or not they were in 'reality' deprived, they would act in a way commensurate with their perceived deprivation. In this way Thomas managed to reduce all social problems to individual ones and to reduce the social structure to individual situations. Analyses of the class structure, the position of women in society and concepts of power and control all become unnecessary in Thomas's work on female criminality. What becomes significant is how the individual reacts to certain micro-level situations and how solutions can be reached by modifying the individual's definition of the situation rather than making structural changes to the social order. Thomas's widest frame of reference is the community which he reifies as an order-maintaining, conservative force preventing the individual from holding deviant definitions of social situations. Moreover he regretted the breakdown of this control, which is based on gossip and intimate contact, caused by rapid urbanization and immigration. As Wright Mills (1943) has pointed out, such a perspective is based on a rural morality which perceives the growth of towns to be fundamentally evil while equating the small rural community or primary group with goodness and order. For Thomas the source of female criminality, which he believed to be mainly sexual, was the breakdown of the traditional restraints on women who formerly would not have thought of working outside the home or marrying outside the ethnic or community group. He stated, for example,

The modern revolt and unrest are due to the contrast between the paucity of fulfillment of the wishes of the individual and the fullness, or apparent fullness, of life around him. All age levels have been affected by the feeling that much, too much, is being missed in life. This unrest is felt most by those who have heretofore been most excluded from general participation in life,—the mature women and the young girl (Thomas, 1967, p. 72).

Because she has been most repressed, therefore, Thomas argued that women are more likely to become 'unadjusted' when social sanctions are removed. Consequently he regretted the passing of a consensus on morality and the growing ambiguity of social norms requiring that individuals make their own moral decisions rather than follow those traditionally laid down by the community.

In conjunction with this overall perspective Thomas was also concerned with the disintegration of the family and the future social adjustment of children. The decline of community support and control in towns and cities meant that social agencies had to be created as replacements and this, Thomas argued, removed any remaining solidarity in the family structure. Yet in spite of such views he was an advocate of the introduction of both the Juvenile Court and pre-delinquency work, two developments which constitute a severe interference in family life. The concept of pre-delinquency work (or the ability to recognize 'criminal tendencies' in the young) in Thomas's work is perhaps the most pernicious aspect of the benevolent liberalism he espoused. The apparently benevolent aspect resided in the fact that children should not be punished like adults for wrongdoing; rather as soon as they were perceived to begin to become 'unadjusted' they should be given guidance and help to achieve 'readjustment'. For example, in discussing the work of the children's bureaux, Thomas stated,

In this work the object has been to work by cases, bringing the girl under the influence of the social worker, improving the home conditions and the attitudes of the parents, placing the girl in a better environment, moving her from one situation to another until one is found to which she responds, and developing in her some activity interest. The ideal is to co-ordinate the girl immediately with the large society in which she lives ... (Thomas, 1967, p. 200).

The pernicious element of the concept of pre-delinquency resides in the mode of assessing signs of delinquency. Usually these signs are the product of middle-class values and a double-standard of morality for males and females. An acceptance of pre-delinquency work also creates a situation in which the 'treatment' of a child becomes justified even if the child has committed no actual offence and moreover the actual 'treatment' given to such children is often indistinguishable from punishment (cf. Platt,

1969). In fact Thomas's liberalism hides a strong authoritarian stance. An example of this authoritarianism is his view that the state should take over the control of children if parents failed to socialize them into the existing social order. The liberal concept of treatment also allows for longer and more severe sentences to be passed on children for criminal and non-criminal offences in order to ensure a 'cure', or rehabilitation. The concept of a trial is also bypassed because the intention of the welfare agencies is not to punish but to help. Thomas was therefore in effect advocating much greater control by the state of the family and children to counteract the decline in community control. His assumption however that there could be a single standard of morality imposed by the state on a diverse urban population ultimately meant the imposition of middle-class values on all sections of society. At the same time as promoting middle-class values by arguing for the readjustment of adolescents and change in the attitudes of parents, Thomas failed to pay any attention to working-class conditions of life. Working-class girls were therefore expected to defer gratification, both sexual and material, even though structurally there was little hope of them ever achieving a middle-class life-style.

Thomas's major failing inasmuch as it concerns us here, however, was his failure to attempt an analysis of the position of women in society and his ignorance of the workings of the double-standard of morality. A girl's or woman's value, according to Thomas, is dependent upon how others perceive her. She has no intrinsic value, she is merely a symbol of purity and she becomes valuable only inasmuch as she pleases and enhances others. Hence Thomas argued that,

The girl as a child does not know she has any particular value until she learns it from others, but if she is regarded with adoration she correspondingly respects herself and tends to become what is expected of her. And so she has in fact a greater value. She makes a better marriage and reflects recognition on her family (Thomas, 1967, p. 98).

A woman is therefore an object of adoration. However, not all women are able to live up to such an ideal of virgin purity and infinite tenderness. Such girls, Thomas argued, are amoral; they are not 'fallen' or immoral, rather they have not had the opportunity to acquire a middle-class moral code and so they cannot be said to have lost it. They will use their sexuality not for its 'appropriate' purpose (i.e. legitimate reproduction) but in order to achieve the material objects or life-styles they desire. This is, according to Thomas, the beginning of their delinquency. However, Thomas overlooked two important structural features of women's lives in his analysis. First, that women were not in the 1920s, nor indeed today, given equal opportunities to earn high salaries or to secure satisfying jobs such that they might buy the material objects they were (and are) encouraged to buy. Consequently selling their labour proved to be far less remunerative than selling their sexuality. Second, he ignored the fact that sexual bargaining is a feature of the lives of all women whilst they are economically dependent on men. Thomas assumed that only girls whose 'natural' sexuality is impaired or underdeveloped could use it in a calculating way for gain. He ignored both the way the 'good' girl must use her virginity to secure a husband and economic security and also the way in which a girl's economic life-chances may be impaired by a lack of virginity. Instead Thomas scrutinized only sexual behaviour which was morally defined as promiscuous, and treating sexual 'deviance' as a sign of individual pathology, he proceeded to construct a causal relationship between a 'defective' self or self-image and sexual nonconformity. Significantly Thomas did not concern himself with the sexual (mis)behaviour of members of the male sex, presumably because the moral code condemns only sexual promiscuity in women. Moreover nowhere in his analysis is there any criticism of a social organization that places such a premium on male sexuality that women and girls can trade their sexuality in return for economic security or gain. Rather the explanation is always in terms of the abnormal or amoral sexuality of women while at the same time it is assumed that promiscuity in men is quite 'natural'.

Thomas's constant theme of adjustment to social norms, which I have argued are mainly middle-class norms, also has particular significance in the study of female delinquency and criminality. His ideological stance encourages the repression of any moves towards a lessening of social constraints on women, emphasizing as it does the conservative, non-criminal nature of the traditional female role. In spite of his recognition of the sacrifices and sublimations necessary in such a role he implicitly supported it and saw the introduction of change as producing undesirable social disorganization. The ultimate morality for Thomas was synonymous with existing social values and the adjustment of the individual to those values. Consequently any challenge to existing social values was perceived not only as dysfunctional but as morally questionable by Thomas. Somewhat inevitably therefore he adopted a highly moralistic tone in his work on female offenders, his moral stance being enhanced by his policy of using anecdotal evidence about the sorry plight of amoral, anomic women in American society. His work in fact contains little analysis but an abundance of descriptive passages which are meant to give weight to his unstructured and uncritical assumptions about the social situation facing immigrant and working-class women. As Wright Mills has pointed out in reference to the standard of work of many American social pathologists,

The level of abstraction which characterizes these texts is so low that often they seem to be empirically confused for lack of abstraction to knit them together. They display bodies of meagerly connected facts, ranging from rape in rural districts to public housing, and intellectually sanction this low level of abstraction (Wright Mills, 1943, p. 166).

Thomas's work is, in this respect, significant to any attempt to trace the development of contemporary attitudes towards female delinquency and criminality (cf. Konopka, 1966). In particular his work has had an impact on social welfare organizations which deal with young, female offenders, because such institutions are concerned with individual cases and situational intervention rather than a theoretical understanding of the relationship between individual behaviour and the entire socio-economic and political structure of society. Thomas's anecdotal style reinforces the antitheoretical stance which is typical of social practitioners, and replacing concern with intellectual understanding, it has encouraged the deflection of the study of female criminality from structural criteria to the realm of the individual emotional and psycho-physiological. The full effect of this influence on the treatment of female offenders will be discussed in Chapter 5.

Otto Pollak

Pollak's study of female criminality, *The Criminality of Women* (1961), reveals the developing influence of sociology, psychology and psychoanalysis on criminology. His work is not classical in a temporal sense because it was originally published at least fifty years after Lombroso and Ferrero's pioneer study. However, Pollak's work is categorized with the works of Lombroso and Ferrero, and Thomas because it reflects a comparable stance and displays the same kind of commonsensical approach to the study of female deviance. Pollak's study does not rely solely on a biological explanation in the way that Lombroso and Ferrero's analysis did; like Thomas he recognizes that social factors are relevant to his project. Nevertheless the attribution of a biological and physiological basis to female criminality is fundamental to his work, as is his culturally loaded, stereotypical perception of members of the female sex. Pollak's study belongs with the classical studies of women and crime primarily because, by sharing their specific world-view and basic methodological assumptions, it fails to develop an understanding of female criminality much beyond the level achieved by Lombroso and Ferrero or Thomas. Indeed his work contains many of the same presuppositions and prejudices, as I shall attempt to demonstrate below, re-presenting them in a modified form. Additionally Pollak's work, in particular his presentation of 'evidence' on the lenient treatment afforded to women, has tended to provide 'confirmation' of a prevalent belief in the 'sympathetic' treatment of female offenders by the police and legal system. Much of his argument has become common currency today and may even be shared by policy-makers and others who become involved with female offenders.[5]

Pollak's major concern is the 'masked' character of female criminality, it being his intention to reveal the 'real' extent and nature of crime committed by women. This 'masked' nature is, according to Pollak, achieved in three ways. First, female criminality is concealed by the under-reporting of offences committed by women; second, by the lower detection rates of female offenders compared to male offenders, and third, by the greater leniency shown to women by the police and courts. Pollak arrives at these explanations as a consequence of his perception of the nature of women and the socio-sexual relations which are an aspect of the social order. It is Pollak's contention that women are the master-minds behind criminal organizations; that they are the instigators of crime rather than the perpetrators; that they can and in fact do manipulate men into committing offences whilst remaining immune from arrest themselves. Such a belief is far from novel, it has its origins in the biblical story of Adam and Eve, and is based on an evaluation of women as possessing an almost supernatural power or extreme cunning which they may utilize for either good or (more usually) evil purposes. Evidence to support this proposition, with the exception of folklore, is however difficult to find, for as Pollak himself points out, such women are rarely apprehended. Yet despite the clear lack of evidence for such a proposition Pollak continues to employ traditional beliefs about the character of women as an unproblematic resource for his analysis.

In addition to making reference to the manipulative powers of women Pollak stresses the inherently deceitful nature of the female sex. He maintains that, 'Man's complaint about woman's deceitfulness is old.... The characterization of greater deceitfulness is, however, by no means confined to criminal women' (Pollak, 1961, pp. 8–9). This legendary deceitfulness is, according to Pollak, socially induced to a certain extent but its origin lies in the female physiology. In particular its source is the passive role assumed by women during sexual intercourse, an inactive role which Pollak clearly believes to be biologically, rather than culturally, determined. He states,

Not enough attention has been paid to the physiological fact that man must achieve an erection in order to perform the sex act and will not be able to hide his failure. His lack of positive emotion in the sexual sphere must become overt to the partner and pretense of sexual response is impossible for him, if it is lacking. Woman's body, however, permits such pretense to a certain degree and lack of orgasm does not prevent her ability to participate in the sex act (Pollak, 1961, p. 10).

The significance, in Pollak's terms, of these 'physiological' differences is the manifestation, on the part of women, of a different attitude towards 'veracity'. Through sexual intercourse, women are able, according to Pollak, to discover and acquire confidence in their ability to deceive men in all respects. As a result Pollak endows all women with the master-status of liars and deceivers because of their ability to conceal a lack of sexual arousal. Thus rather than considering the implications of the sexual politics which produce a situation in which many women endure intercourse when they are neither aroused nor acquiescent, Pollak takes the existence of a passive engagement in sexual activity as a basis of assumptions about women's ambiguous attitude towards honesty and deceit. He fails to consider, for example, that on marriage women sacrifice their legal rights to sexual self-determination to their spouses and that (at one time) a refusal to allow a husband sexual access was considered adequate grounds for divorce. Pollak is in fact oblivious to the existing imbalance of power between men and women, as well as the differences in cultural expectations concerning acceptable behaviour in the sexual realm. Rather than considering such differences as topics of analysis relevant to his study, Pollak prefers to treat them as confirming the accuracy of folklore and stereotypical perceptions of women.

The masked nature of female criminality is not merely treated as a reflection of the cunning deceit of women however; it is also for Pollak a result of the fact that the typical victims of crimes committed by women do not report offences to the police. Pollak argues that the female offender's usual victim is her lover, husband or children, and indeed where violence is concerned this has been substantiated (Wolfgang, 1958; Ward et al., 1969). Further, as far as reporting offences is concerned, Pollak is probably quite correct, especially in the case of crimes committed against children, for it is likely that children (given the existing power structure of the family) do not report offences of violence against themselves by their parents. But Pollak overlooks the fact that fathers may also abuse their children and that, within the privacy of the home, many women are themselves the secret victims of their husbands' aggression. Instead Pollak maintains that when women are the victims of assault by men they will readily go to the police and prosecute their assailants whereas when men are the victims of female aggression there is a great deal of reticence to report the offence. Thus he argues that assaults by women are under-reported while assaults by men are not. Clearly such attempts to estimate the comparative degree of hidden male and female crime are purely speculative and the basis for Pollak's belief that female criminality is more 'masked' than male criminality is insubstantial. Pollak has virtually no evidence and relies instead upon tenuous assumptions about the behaviour of men and women which clearly do not constitute sufficient grounds for his assertions. In addition the availability of conflicting evidence such as the widespread occurrence of wife-battering, which is indicative of the 'masked' nature of assaults by men, suggests that hidden male criminality may well be just as significant, may assume a similar form and may occur in a similar context to hidden female criminality.

The final significant factor proposed by Pollak in accounting for the hidden quality of female criminality is the existence of chivalry on the part of men towards women. He argues that men have deceived themselves about women; have treated women as docile and in need of protection because they fear insurrection by women who are forced into an unequal place in society. And because of this self-deception Pollak argues that men have found it hard to believe that women could be criminal and so have failed to report, charge and convict women for the many offences they engage in. He states,

Basically they have attempted to deny women the ability to do things men do and have either idealized them into a sweetness and purity which made them appear docile and harmless, or they have maligned them in order to be able to condemn them (Pollak, 1961, p. 149).

However, in spite of an apparent recognition of the darker side of chivalry and the possibility of scapegoating the 'fallen' woman, Pollak neglects to incorporate these elements into his study. He only discusses the way in which discrimination against women by the courts and police can serve in the interest of women, he ignores the other possibility that some women (especially prostitutes or other so-called sexual deviants) may be used as scapegoats and hence negatively discriminated against.

In fact Pollak is not unaware of the existence of a double standard of morality for men and women, nor of the social and sexual repression of women in general. Yet he is not critical of such an inequitable social order; rather it serves as merely another causal factor in his study. For example he suggests that because women are repressed they look for ways of avenging themselves on those men whom they perceive to be the cause of their inferior status. This vengeance may take the form of false accusations, perjury, arson or even murder and assault. In this respect Pollak's analysis bears strong resemblance to Lombroso and Ferrero's study for both appear to be convinced that when 'roused' women are far more dangerous than men. Pollak's revision of this aspect of folklore is supplemented with statistical data which are presented as evidence for the proposition that female offenders are more murderous and violent than men once they graduate beyond the level of petty crimes. Using data on the commitments of female offenders to federal and state institutions for murder and manslaughter in 1940, Pollak maintains that female offenders committed for these offences constitute 11·9 per cent of all female commitments. The commitments for male offenders for these crimes constitute only 4·9 per cent of all male commitments, however. Consequently he finds that women have a greater liability for homicides. He makes similar computations for commitments for aggravated assaults and finds female offenders represent 8·6 per cent of all female commitments to prison while male offenders represent only 5·1 per cent of male commitments. This use of statistical data and the comparisons he makes are however methodologically unsound and totally misleading. In absolute terms there are (and were when Pollak was writing) far fewer women in prison than men. Pollak himself has given many reasons for this and whether or not his speculations about how much female crime remains undetected are valid it is reasonable to assume, even accepting all the qualifications surrounding official statistics, that women commit some crimes less frequently than men. In other words it may be argued for example that because of a lack of illegitimate opportunities fewer women than men are likely to commit certain forms of larceny and other offences against property. On the other hand women do appear to be involved to a large extent in petty offences which do not necessarily lead to imprisonment if they are first offenders. Consequently there are likely to be fewer women than men in prison for property offences of a relatively serious or even a petty nature. On the other hand it is far less likely that murderers and violent offenders will escape imprisonment if they are convicted because such offences are rarely treated with great leniency and tend to lead to a sentence of imprisonment. Women offenders committing serious violent crimes are therefore unlikely to escape imprisonment and consequently these violent offenders will not be as under-represented in our prison population as less serious offenders. As a result of this the number of women in prison *in toto* is likely to contain proportionately more serious violent offenders compared to other offenders than is the case for the male prison population. Thus the evidence cited by Pollak is explicable in terms other than the greater murderous intent or violence of female offenders. Similarly the small proportions of male offenders committed for homicide and assault are not necessarily indicative of the non-violence of male offenders but are more likely to be indicative of the relatively greater statistical significance of the other offences they commit which lead to imprisonment.

Pollak's fundamental reliance on biological and physiological factors (in association with social factors) as a basis for an explanation of female criminality has been considered. His recourse to biology often serves as a way of explaining the social and psychological influence of physiological processes or abnormalities. Implicit in this method is an attempt to show that there is some biological, psychic or social imbalance present in women when they commit criminal offences. In particular Pollak lays stress on the so-called 'generative' phases, namely menstruation, pregnancy and the menopause. He states that

The student of female criminality cannot afford to overlook the generally known and recognized fact that these generative phases are frequently accompanied·by psychological disturbances which may upset the need and satisfaction balance of the individual or weaken her internal inhibitions, and thus become causative factors in female crime (Pollak, 1961, p. 157).

The concepts of a 'need and satisfaction balance' or 'internal inhibitions' are reminiscent of a biological automaton which cannot think or reason but which merely reacts according to stimuli. Yet Pollak is not quite as deterministic as this for he does seek to explain the psychological and social impact on women of menstruation and other bodily changes. These explanations are not necessarily more acceptable though, for he accounts for crime during menstruation as an act of vengeance by women for the confirmation of their inferior status. His understanding of women's relationship to their own biology is very much influenced by Freudian analysis and he assumes an association between the menstrual cycle, the ultimate failure to become a man (it being assumed that all women desire to be men) and sexual guilt. The menopause on the other hand is associated with the loss of womanhood which induces depression, irritability and consequently crime. In spite of a lack of any substantial empirical evidence to substantiate such hypotheses these explanations of female criminality are still in vogue (Dalton, 1961; Gibbens and Prince, 1962). This search for a simple causal factor in female crime which Pollak promotes is indicative of the low level of theoretical achievement and the retarded nature of most studies in this area. It is also indicative of a certain attitude towards women which infers that simple, biologically-based, causal factors can explain the motivation and reasoning of complex, culturally located and socially meaningful acts.

In the conclusion to his study of female criminality Pollak states, 'In our male-dominated culture, women have always been considered as strange, secretive and sometimes as dangerous' (Pollak, 1961, p. 149). Unfortunately he has done little to dispel these myths, rather he has incorporated them into his analysis and has thereby given folklore a pseudo-scientific status.

Chapter 3

Contemporary studies of female criminality

In my exposition of the classical studies of female criminality I made reference to their continuing influence on the development of analyses of criminality and delinquency by contemporary criminologists. In this chapter I will fully examine the nature of this influence through a critical appraisal of the works of Cowie, Cowie and Slater (1968) and Konopka (1966) both of which are representative of studies of female criminality carried out in recent decades. In addition I will examine recent attempts to extricate the study of female criminality from its traditional containment within a biological, psychological and medical science oriented problematic and will go on to consider the increasingly predominant and persuasive argument that female emancipation has produced changes in the criminal behaviour of women. Now the emancipation argument is not contemporary in origin[1] and if we are to understand its re-emergence at this historical moment as a popular explanation of the perceived increase in delinquency amongst girls and the resort to so-called 'unfeminine' styles of crime by women, we need to consider critically both the actual effect of specific social changes on the position of women and the prevalent belief that such changes have actually enabled women to achieve equality with men in all the important spheres of social life.

Cowie, Cowie and Slater

Cowie, Cowie and Slater's study, *Delinquency in Girls* (1968), is a contemporary work which has remained very close to the positivist tradition of Lombroso. Although they have clearly rejected the naïve concept of atavism there are two significant features in their analysis which bear a strong resemblance to Lombroso and Ferrero's approach. First, they have retained the view that criminality is a sign of pathology, an abnormal occurrence which can be eliminated if the causal factors are isolated. Hence in their project Cowie *et al.* engage in a search for the variables which will enable them to distinguish between the delinquent (or potentially delinquent) girl and the non–delinquent (or normal) girl. In particular they look for signs of 'defective' intelligence, abnormal central nervous function and impaired physical health. Their findings reveal that 'Delinquent girls more often than boys have other forms of impaired physical health; they are noticed to be oversized, lumpish, uncouth and graceless, with a raised incidence of minor physical defects' (Cowie *et al.*, 1968, pp. 166–7). These observations bear an uncanny resemblance to Lombroso's descriptions of criminal women. Yet they are not mere descriptions because Cowie *et al.* treat these features as 'constitutional predisposing factors' to delinquency. Unfortunately they do not begin to consider the social processes which differentially produce characteristics such as these in members of specific social groups. In particular they are sublimely unaware of the social class bias which is implicit in their institutionalized sample, the fact that less affluent members of society may have less satisfactory diets, poorer medical care and less opportunity to satisfactorily meet the stereotypical middle-class normative standard of appearance for adolescent girls. Amongst the other predisposing factors identified by Cowie *et al.* is a deprived childhood, a deprivation appearing to hinge mainly on maternal deprivation although it is recognized that in a minority of cases incestuous fathers may play a role in predisposing a girl to delinquency.

There is a tendency in the work of Cowie, Cowie and Slater to relegate social and environmental factors to insignificance in comparison to physiological and psychological criteria. In spite of the fact that they maintain that they discovered disruptive social and environmental factors in half of the biographies of the delinquent girls they studied such factors are not attributed with much significance in predisposing girls to become delinquent. This is because Cowie *et al.* argue that the female sex is more 'immune' to delinquency than the male sex even where environmental factors can be said to be criminogenic. In other words Cowie *et al.* invoke a biological determinist model (in a way similar to that of Lombroso and Ferrero), maintaining that the biological difference between the sexes represents the most significant cause of the difference in the nature and frequency of crimes committed by men and women. Thus it is implied that girls will only become delinquent when they are biologically abnormal or where a minor abnormality (i.e. overweight) is combined with extremely stressful environmental factors. They argue that girls are far less affected by social circumstances than boys so that while social and economic explanations may well be appropriate in accounting for delinquency in boys, for girls delinquent behaviour requires a biological explanation. For example, Cowie *et al.* maintain that 'The pattern of development in personality and behaviour is more stable and more consistent in the female than in the male, and can take a larger stress before being disrupted' (Cowie *et al.*, 1968, pp. 176–7). Female delinquency and criminality is therefore seen in terms of the biological constitution of the female sex. Women and girls do not participate to any great extent in violence, robbery or fraud for example, primarily because of their chromosomal and hormonal physiological structure, not because of a lack of illicit opportunity or more rigid social control. It is in this respect that Cowie *et al.* bear a second close resemblance to Lombroso and Ferrero, who insisted that social factors merely channel abnormal or pathological biological states. The problem that this biological determinist position creates however is how to explain the way in which physiological structures can give rise to social action, in particular social action that is culturally (not biologically) defined as delinquent or criminal. Biological determinist accounts beg two questions: first, what form does the relationship between such things as genes, chromosomes or body shape and crime and delinquency assume, and second, in what respects, if any, can deviant behaviour or criminal activity be considered independently of the associated defining agencies and legal processes, independently, that is, of the social construction of laws and mores? The biological determinist position treats the existence of criminal laws as given and takes the legal definition of criminality as its basis; consequently there is no consideration of the ways in which criminal laws 'create' criminals or of the specific sectional interests of the existing criminal law. The neutrality of the law is taken for granted and the processes by which individuals become, or become to be seen as, criminal remains unconsidered.

Cowie, Cowie and Slater give virtually no attention to the socio-cultural basis of definitions of criminal and deviant behaviour nor do they appear to recognize the significance of power in the framing and enforcement of laws and social norms. They are aware of the existence of a double-standard of morality but this awareness in no way informs their analysis of female delinquency, which in fact they accept as being mainly sexual in character. Where they do attempt to deal with the question posed by the behavioural manifestations of physiological differences their argument is couched in terms of the chromosomal structure of the sexes, the 'normal' female having two X chromosomes and the 'normal' male having one X and one Y chromosome. Their thesis is that delinquency is related to the Y chromosome, it being argued that males with an extra Y chromosome are more common amongst criminals than amongst the average population. The specific limitations of this type of chromosomal thesis are outlined elsewhere[2] and therefore do not require exposition here. In any case the thesis advanced by Cowie et al. is not primarily dependent upon the validity of the XYY thesis, the controversial nature of which they avoid by stating that 'A simple and obvious hypothesis is that the Y chromosome merely determines the development of a masculine pattern of psychosomatic constitution, and that it is this masculinity as such that predisposes to delinquency, and predisposes to masculine types of delinquency' (Cowie et al., 1968, p. 171). Hence they argue that the Y chromosome determines masculinity and that masculinity predisposes individuals to delinquency. Thus if masculinity, which is biologically determined according to Cowie et al., is a prerequisite for delinquency it follows that female delinquents may have an abnormal chromosomal structure, for they have demonstrated masculine attributes by participating in delinquent activity. Thus Cowie et al. ask

Is there any evidence that *masculinity or femininity of bodily constitution* plays any part [*sic*] predisposing to delinquency and in determining the form it takes? (Cowie *et al.*, 1968, p. 171). (Emphasis added.)

And in reply they maintain,

Delinquents of both sexes tend to be larger than controls, and overgrown by population standards.... Markedly masculine traits in girl delinquents have been commented on by psycho-analytical observers ... We can be sure that they have some *physical basis* (op. cit., 1968, pp. 171–2). (Emphasis added.)

Although they express certainty that an abnormal chromosomal balance is at the root of female delinquency no medical evidence exists to support this hypothesis. But a more significant flaw in the logic of their argument is their neglect or ignorance of the distinction between sex and gender. Like Lombroso and Ferrero they assume that sex is biologically determined and that gender is also immutably fixed. Thus they proceed to argue that, for a girl to display masculine forms of behaviour, which might be termed gender inappropriate, she must have an overbalance of male chromosomes.

They do not perceive gender roles to be at all fluid, insisting that femininity is a *natural* attribute of the female and that masculinity is similarly *natural* for the male. They entirely overlook the way in which different cultures produce different forms of gender-appropriate behaviour such that women in some societies[3] may adopt what would be defined as masculine behaviour in our own culture. Instead they assume that for a girl to adopt typically masculine behaviour is symbolic of a biological abnormality. They assume that there is only one form of behaviour which is *natural* for the female sex and that that form is biologically determined. Moreover this form of behaviour is held to exclude delinquency and criminality with the consequence that any evidence of non-conformity in girls and women is treated as a sure sign of pathology. In their analysis, Cowie *et al.* are unable to conceive of the female sex outside of the traditional, stereotypical roles. They insist that women are protected from delinquency because 'the female mode of personality [is] more prudent, more timid, more lacking in enterprise'. Thus they assume that there is only one 'mode of personality' natural to the female sex and they associate stereotypical, gender-appropriate behaviour with the 'true' nature of the female sex. Therefore, like Lombroso and Ferrero, they promote the culturally-specific to the level of the 'natural' or biologically ordained. They do not attempt to analyse the type of social structure which condemns signs of 'enterprise', adventurousness or independence in its female members and imposes a system of dependency and impotence within which women are expected to find self-fulfilment. Neither do they appear to appreciate the way in which their treatment of woman as a passive, nurturing conservative being tacitly supports the cultural model of man as an active, aggressive and creative being. In this respect their analysis cannot be differentiated from their predecessors Lombroso and Ferrero, and Thomas.

These failings in Cowie, Cowie and Slater's work stem from their acceptance of the culturally given appearance of reality as a basis for analysis and from their reliance on a common-sense perspective which eschews any critical theoretical framework. Thus they treat the study of female delinquency in isolation from all social institutions, the one exception being the family. This practice serves in fact increasingly to mystify the phenomenon under study by excluding from analysis all the other agencies involved in the creation of deviancy (e.g. police, courts and social workers). Their approach is then predicated upon the assumption that deviance can be understood apart from its cultural context; it is an approach which seeks to confirm rather than critically examine prevailing understandings of female criminality; hence their continual appeal to the student's 'senses' and 'feelings', rather than reason, for confirmation of analysis. Indeed Cowie *et al.*, rather than relying on credible, scientific evidence, evoke 'common-sense' and the 'natural' as support for their explanations of female delinquency. For example they maintain:

It is more *natural* to suppose that the male-female difference, both in delinquency rates and in the forms that delinquency takes, would be closely connected with the masculine or

59

feminine pattern of development of personality (op. cit., 1968, p. 170). (Emphasis added.)

And again later they state:

Common-sense suggests that the main factors [in predisposing to delinquency] are somatic ones, especially hormonal ones . . . (op. cit., 1968, p. 171). (Emphasis added.)

Significantly Cowie *et al.* do not attempt to analyse critically common-sense understandings of sexuality, sexual differences or female delinquency; they accept them as if they constituted the basis of objective evidence and in consequence they fail to see the cultural and historical limitations of their work or its ideological function. As a result of these limitations Cowie *et al.* fail to appreciate the diversity of the social phenomenon they are studying and ultimately they present a mere description of culturally-given beliefs about female delinquency in the guise of an analytical explanation. Their appeal to common sense has however other far-reaching consequences, for it serves to perpetuate and give scientific credibility to folklore and myth, thereby further mystifying our understanding of deviant phenomena. By accepting and taking for granted the parameters inherent in prevailing cultural understandings of female delinquency Cowie *et al.*'s work appears to be of immediate practical value. In adhering to the pre-given, pre-defined character of female delinquency (as based upon the legal definition) their work is oriented towards the provision of knowledge and the production of social control technologies which makes possible the prevention or cure of delinquent behaviour in girls considered as individual pathological cases. In so far as they reduce the significance of social or environmental factors, neglect to analyse the social processes underlying the given behaviour and its classification as deviant, their work bears a strong resemblance to Lombroso and Ferrero's analysis of crimes committed by women. Cowie, Cowie and Slater may therefore be recognized as contemporary counterparts to Lombroso, their work representing a reformulation and development of the same ideological ingredients informing Lombroso and Ferrero's study of female criminality.

G. Konopka

Gisela Konopka's study, *The Adolescent Girl in Conflict* (1966), displays the influence of W. I. Thomas and the liberal tradition within criminology rather than the biological positivism of Lombroso and Ferrero. This influence is particularly noticeable in Konopka's style of presentation because, like Thomas, her work is descriptive rather than analytical, having a strong reliance on anecdotal evidence and individual case histories. Konopka's study is full of the records of private and personal conversations that she had with institutionalized delinquent girls and the reports of social workers are a major part of her descriptions of the misery and loneliness experienced by these girls. In this way Konopka attempts to evoke sympathy for the delinquent girl and to disturb the conscience of the readers, making them aware of our failure to understand the problems of adolescent girls as well as our failure to provide adequate treatment or care for girls once they have become delinquent. It is because of her obvious concern for the care of delinquent girls that Konopka's work is particularly influential in the realms of social work and the 'caring' professions. In this respect she is within the same tradition as Thomas and more contemporary writers like Vedder and Sommerville (1970) who address themselves specifically to the problem of social intervention and the furtherance of techniques of behaviour modification and social control. This orientation towards the 'treatment' of the individual delinquent is founded upon the prevalent belief that delinquency or criminality are signs of individual maladjustment. Furthermore, Konopka's emphasis on individual case histories strengthens this perception because her method stresses the individuality of delinquents, while overlooking the similarities in their structural position within society, and also emphasizes the significance of personal problems and inadequacies as opposed to social factors such as poverty, the unequal distribution of wealth and differential opportunity structures. It is not the case that Konopka is unaware of these structural factors however but rather that she treats them as aggravations to, or causes of, personal maladjustment instead of realizing that so-called delinquent behaviour may be rational, meaningful behaviour within a given context. It is significant also that Konopka does not question the legal framework which defines delinquents but accepts that those girls so labelled are in fact delinquent. This is in spite of her awareness that double standards of morality operate in the defining process thereby making any deviant act (especially sexual) by a girl appear more serious than a comparable act by a boy and therefore more likely to result in a delinquent label. Perhaps most surprising is the way in which Konopka appears to assume that institutionalized girls are representative of all delinquent girls and proceeds to treat their case histories and individual problems as characteristic of delinquency as a whole. Like the early studies of male delinquency, it is implicit in her work that all delinquents come from poor or broken homes with insufficient parental guidance and a lack of education. As a consequence her study is situated within the limited framework of the legal definition of delinquency and she gives no attention to the way in which certain members of society become defined as delinquent or are confirmed in their criminal/delinquent statuses.

The descriptive nature of Konopka's work poses yet another problem to our understanding of female criminality. This problem hinges upon the fact that Konopka treats the ability to describe an event or process as though it is free from either individual or cultural interpretation. She treats the subject of her study as an unproblematic 'real-in-the-world' fact which is self-evident to any observer. Thus, using a tape recorder and her own notes of conversations, she maintains that she merely re-presents reality to us without interpretation or, as she describes it, without bias. Yet she has had to be selective in sorting out which excerpts to present to us, as she readily admits she has many files full of material remaining unpublished. Unfortunately the criteria she has employed in her selection process are not revealed let alone clarified or justified. Indeed Konopka claims that she has no preconceived criteria or theoretical framework and argues that such 'tools' should only be implemented after the collation of material. But her faith in the possibility of non-interpretative methods of collecting information is based on a fallacy. In effect she is arguing that it is possible to enter a social situation with the intention of obtaining information without that information which is being collected being influenced by the biographical relevances of the investigator, their existing knowledge, or the interpretative procedures necessarily employed by anybody to make sense of any social encounter. She rejects theory, and yet if in its broadest sense, theorizing is taken to be a mode of conceptualizing that is rationally based on existing knowledge, her rejection becomes an attempt to understand without any rational powers of comprehension. Hindess has clearly outlined the absurdity of such a position in his critique of positivist methodology. He states that

If we were to send into the field a team of ideal observers, stripped of all concepts (to avoid the possible influence of alien categories), they would return with nothing to report and no vocabulary with which to report it. Any proposed set of categories can only be evaluated in terms of existing knowledge, knowledge that is always already a product of some means of production of knowledge (Hindess, 1973, p. 40).

Konopka's attempt to avoid what she perceived as bias by employing theory only after observation is a clear case of self-deception. It means that she fails to explicate her interpretative criteria and in consequence we are presented with a study which is based on selections made from conversational materials and personal observations which Konopka treats as having an objective factual status. Unfortunately, contrary to Konopka's assumptions, observation and understanding involve selection and interpretation and are not free from pre-conceptualization, no interpretative process can be. The observation of 'facts' is not unproblematical as Konopka seems to imagine; facts are socially created; they do not have an independent existence in the world. A social fact is not an inherently independent, externally existent object, it is the outcome of a determinate social process, a production process involving interpretation of an event and knowledge of the social context in which the specific event occurs. In the case of Konopka's work no attention is given to these difficulties; rather communication between researcher, 'delinquent' and reader is assumed to be free and undistorted. Konopka's failure to appreciate the methodological complexity of social inquiry and her reduction of delinquency to an emotional problem, coupled with her assumptions about the inherent 'needs' of the female sex, results in a study which is as limited in its insights as the classical studies of female criminality.

The treatment of delinquency as an individual problem is not only a consequence of Konopka's inadequate comprehension of social science methodology preventing her from going beyond the description of individual or small group situations, it is also a reflection of the tradition within criminology which insists on treating deviancy as an individual problem and not a structurally produced phenomenon. In consequence the causal basis of delinquency has frequently been defined as psychological. Three main factors may be identified for the emergence of this kind of explanation. First, the increasing influence of psychological explanations which have begun to replace purely biological analyses; second, the liberal tradition within which Konopka works which stresses the needs of individuals with the benevolent intention of supplying more effective treatment, and third, the assumption that emotionality is an inherent failure of the female sex. The psychological explanations which form the cornerstone of many contemporary accounts of female criminality (especially prostitution; see Chapter 4) originate with the Freudian theory of child-parent relationships and oedipal conflicts. They are supplemented by the maternal deprivation thesis which emphasizes the necessity of continuous maternal love if well-adjusted, conforming societal members are to be produced. Konopka places great stress on an apparent absence of love in the home lives of the girls in her study and she perceives this absence as a precipitating factor in the emotional instability and subsequent (sexual) delinquency of the girls. Implicit here is the assumption that one must be unstable or unbalanced to become delinquent, a 'normal' well-adjusted girl by definition is not, and cannot become, delinquent. It does not occur to Konopka that if emotional instability exists in the delinquent girls she studied, such instability might be a criteria for institutionalization rather than a factor which predisposes to delinquency.

The interest underlying the liberal tradition in criminology, which is exemplified by Konopka, is the production of a body of literature[4] to assist the caring professions in the recognition of basic human needs which are unsatisfied and the provision of therapy and treatment programmes. The treatment that is supplied however is geared towards adjusting the individual to fit into her or his personal situation rather than to radically changing social structure such that problem-creating situations are themselves remedied. The concentration on the individual leaves the politico-economic structure intact and improves methods of controlling deviant members by providing more efficient social services. This is particularly pertinent for deviants who are members of the female sex because of the common assumption, which is present in Konopka's study, that women and girls have special and intense personal needs which may lead to anti-social or criminal behaviour if they are not fully satisfied. These needs are for love, protection and dependency. As Konopka states,

Adolescent boys, too, often feel lonely and search for under-standing and friends. Yet, in general, this does not seem to be the central core of their problems, not their most outspoken ache. While these girls also strive for independence, their need for *dependence* is unusually great—and almost completely over-looked and unfulfilled. This need for support seems to exist in all adolescent girls ... (Konopka, 1966, pp. 40–1).

My criticism of Konopka's assumptions about the special needs of adolescent girls hinges on the meaning of the concept 'need'. Because of her psychological orientation it becomes apparent that she means inherent needs rather than culturally determinate needs. She does not address the nature and form of social structures which place women in a subordinate and dependent position, thereby ensuring that the majority of girls and women will indeed require material and psychological support and protection as a result of the structural limitation of access to the psychic and material resources necessary to provide for self-sufficiency and independence. Konopka's analysis of the emotional needs of women is in fact very close to Thomas's own theory of 'wishes' in which he argued that women have an inherently greater need for emotional response or love than men. Neither Thomas nor Konopka considers the cultural pressures on men that cause them to suppress or disguise their emotions for fear of being labelled weak or effeminate, nor for that matter do they consider the cultural acceptance and expectation of displays of emotion in women. Consequently they perpetuate prevailing perceptions and thereby fail to advance our understanding of the basis of gender differences and their relationship to criminality. Konopka can be seen therefore to be engaged in a process of weaving taken-for-granted assumptions about the female sex into an explanation of juvenile delinquency and in this respect her analysis, like that of Cowie, Cowie and Slater, ultimately fails to demystify the study of female criminality.

Role theory

The explanation of female criminality in terms of the social differentiation of gender roles represents one of the first real attempts to analyse this phenomenon in other than biological or psychological terms. The theorists who have recognized the limitations of the traditional modes of analysis (cf. Heidensohn, 1968; Hoffman-Bustamante, 1973; Rosenblum, 1975) have proceeded by examining the significance of such factors as differential socialization, differential illegitimate opportunity structures and differential social reaction, to an explanation of female deviance. For example Hoffman-Bustamante emphasizes the existence of culturally different methods of socializing girls and boys in advanced industrialized Western society. Girls are generally more closely supervised than boys and are taught to be passive and domesticated while boys are allowed greater freedom and are encouraged to be aggressive, ambitious and outward going. Clearly this pattern of socialization will vary to a certain degree, especially in different socio-economic classes where cultural attitudes and values may vary, but this does not detract from the fact that both socialization and the later development of consciousness and self-perception does vary considerably between the sexes. As a result of this girls are usually expected to be non-violent and so are not allowed to learn how to fight or use weapons. Girls themselves tend to shrink from violence and look for protection rather than seeking to learn the skills of self-defence, hence few women have the necessary technical ability or strength to engage in crimes of violence, armed robberies or gang fights. Even where women do participate in such crimes their method of involvement appears to reflect their gender role and socialization. For example with homicides, women have been found most frequently to kill their relatives or lovers, using a minimum of violence, and most usually using a kitchen implement such as a knife (Wolfgang, 1958). All the available data on violent crimes by women appear to reflect the domestic world in which women still predominate and the use of such a weapon as the knife indicates familiarity with a weapon which is more usually a domestic tool. In the case of offences like burglary or robbery, Hoffman-Bustamante maintains 'it appears that they have played secondary, supportive roles. . . . Thus, women seem to commit crimes in roles auxiliary to men, in keeping with their sex roles and for lesser returns; often making them more vulnerable to arrest' (Hoffman-Bustamante, 1973, p. 131). Consequently the differential socialization of girls is reflected not only in the types of offences committed by women but also in the nature of their participation.

Different expectations of standards of behaviour also appear to be significant in the production of female criminality. Where it is more heavily impressed on girls (than boys) that certain types of behaviour are morally wrong or inappropriate it seems likely that a greater level of conformity will result or, failing that, a stronger feeling of guilt will accompany deviant action. It also follows that because girls are expected to abide by stricter moral standards they will condemn more readily a failure to conform in others. Morris (1965) has attempted to test these assumptions to discover the nature of the relationship between the sexes and attitudes towards non-conformity. Her findings indicate that there is more shame felt by girls than boys when they are questioned about having been in trouble with the police. Morris defined shame in terms of an unwillingness on the part of respondents to admit to an involvement with the police even though it had been officially recorded and in certain cases was common knowledge among the respondent's peers. This study provides an apparent confirmation of typical role expectations for boys and girls; boys who are generally expected to be mischievous were able to boast of their enterprises while girls were more reluctant to admit to their deviant behaviour.

Morris also found that the girls were more critical than the boys of delinquency in general and this critical attitude may be interpreted as a greater protection for girls from the pressures of delinquency. It is however unwise to rely too extensively on the results of Morris's study for it is well known that what people *say* about their thoughts and actions, especially in interviews, is not always synonymous with what they think and do in other social situations. The girls in Morris's sample may merely have been responding to what they saw as the expectation of conformity and their replies may have been oriented towards a display of compliance rather than representative of an accurate report of intentions or actions. Nevertheless, in spite of the difficulty of assessing people's attitudes to deviant behaviour, it is probable that the lower involvement of girls in delinquency continues to be primarily related to existing socialization patterns, in particular the greater restrictions placed on the freedom of movement of most girls at the age when their male peers are 'discovering' delinquency. So whether or not girls actually do conform to gender-appropriate attitudes towards delinquency and criminality their ability to participate is structurally restricted. The realization of a lack of access to illegitimate opportunity structures for adolescent girls and women is of course a most perceptive insight into an understanding of female criminality. Even though it may appear to be self-evident that members of the female sex have been denied the opportunity to engage in anything other than petty or domestic offences the traditional approaches to the study of female criminality have consistently overlooked these structural factors in favour of theories based on physiological or psychological predispositions and causes. In accounting for the insignificance of female criminality these theories are similar to those explanations which seek to account for the virtual absence of great female scientists, artists, composers and philosophers in terms of predetermined biological and psychic differences and the existence of an alternative field of (pro)creativity for women. However, although the rejection of biological and psychological determinism is an important development in our understanding of female criminality, structural limitations on illegitimate opportunities cannot alone provide a sufficient explanation to account for the differences between female and male criminality. For example, as I will show later, differential societal reaction plays an important part in determining which forms of female behaviour are treated as delinquent or criminal and in differentially defining behaviour as deviant according to the sex of the offender.

The study of female criminality in terms of gender roles cannot be, and to be fair, is probably not intended to provide a complete analysis of the phenomenon. Unfortunately however its partial and incomplete grasp of the problem produces two major limitations. First, there is a failure to situate the discussion of sex roles within a structural explanation of the social origins of those roles. In other words, there is no attempt to account for the development of the division of labour between the sexes nor to explain the socially inferior nature of women's status and position in historical, economic or cultural terms. Consequently the role theorists do not substantially challenge the prevailing belief that sex roles and gender differences are 'natural', that is biologically determined. This serious omission allows those who adhere to biological determinist or positivist perspectives to employ role theory as a further 'proof' of the validity of their own explanations of the basis of sexual differentiation. Second, role theory fails to discuss motivation or intention as an integral part of female criminality. For example role theory does not explain why, even though women are socialized into primarily conforming patterns of behaviour, a considerable number engage in crime. By concentrating on why women do not commit offences role theory leaves the explanation of why some women offend to the traditional positivist theories. Consequently the question that role theory fails to address adequately leaves open the opportunity for explanations in terms of poor or unsuccessful socialization or role-frustration. The 'poor socialization' thesis is based on a belief in an ordered consensual social order in which the interests of the individual or minority group are synonymous with those of the whole of society or more appropriately the ruling order. Poor socialization as an explanation of female deviance implies a pathology existing within the individual which requires treatment rather than a conception of deviance as a structurally produced, conflict situation. On the other hand the role frustration thesis implies that the basic cause of deviance is psychological and emotional. It suggests that some women are overcome by the frustrations of their limiting sex role and so turn to crime as a means of relief. But frustration and emotion may equally lead to legitimate channels of relief; they do not necessarily and inevitably give rise to what are socially defined as criminal acts. Frustration tends to be a 'catch-all' explanation which, because it seems to be employed to explain anything, actually explains nothing.

Role theory therefore is of limited value in accounting for female criminality. To improve the status of the role theory approach the concept of role must itself be located within a theory which first can account for the existence of specifically differentiated roles as well as other features of human activity (like criminality) and second treats *both* as the outcome of socio-economic, political and historical factors, rather than treating one (crime) as the outcome of the other (sex roles).

Women's emancipation and the increase in crime

One assumption that is implicit in the role theorist's account of female criminality is that, as women's roles change and become more open to the opportunities and tensions associated with the male role, more women will engage more frequently in crime. The underlying fear of the detrimental consequences to law and order concomitant with the emancipation of women is not however new. Lombroso, for one, spoke of the dangers of educating women and removing the constraints of domesticity and maternity which he maintained would allow the 'innocuous semi-criminal' present in all women to emerge. Similarly, W. I. Thomas quoted a passage from the *New York World*, published in 1921, which places the responsibility for most social ills on the 'doorstep' of the Women's Movement. It reads:

The modern age of girls and young men is intensely immoral, and immoral seemingly without the pressure of circumstances. At whose door we may lay the fault, we cannot tell. Is it the result of what we call 'the emancipation of woman', with its concomitant freedom from chaperonage, increased intimacy between the sexes in adolescence, and a more tolerant viewpoint towards all things unclean in life? This seems the only logical forbear of the present state (Thomas, 1961, pp. 84–5).

The Women's Movement appears to have struck immense fear into the hearts of criminologists for generations past, even when the demands of such a movement were modest compared with the claims for equality made today. As the Movement has now re-emerged and re-asserted itself again, it is being conceived once more as a threat to the stable character of female criminality and contemporary observers may be found to be expressing similar comments to Lombroso and Thomas about the dangers of allowing women the same 'freedoms' as men. For example, in the Staff Report submitted to the US National Commission on the Causes and Prevention of Violence, it is stated that

It is also the case that the 'emancipation' of females in our society over recent decades has decreased the differences in delinquency and criminality between boys and girls, men and women, as cultural differences between them have narrowed (Mulvihill *et al.*, 1969, p. 425).

While in a paper presented at the Institute for the Study and Treatment of Delinquency's annual conference in the UK, it was asserted that

perhaps some of the problem is to do with uni-sex, the seeking by the girl for equality with the man, in every way including violence, ... I think this is true. No longer can you appeal to the girls, as in the past, on grounds of femininity, or of being feminine—that has no meaning at all ... (Hart, 1975, p. 7).

It appears to be generally accepted that there is a direct causal relationship between female emancipation, or what Hart strangely terms 'uni-sex', and what is perceived to be a new trend in female criminality. The emancipation argument therefore may be seen to hinge upon two major premises, first, that offences committed by girls and women are becoming more 'masculine', in particular more violent, and second, that the Women's Movement represents an attempt to emulate the male sex, or at least a convergence of the sexes (the former being the most common assumption). I shall deal with these two premises separately.

The first premise is based on changes in the official statistics which seem to indicate that the involvement of women in crime is increasing rapidly. The question is however whether the increase in offences by females is increasing at a proportionately higher rate than offences by males. There is a considerable debate on this point: Heidensohn (1968) for example argues that the rate for sexual offences by women is declining and that overall the proportionate increase in the conviction rate for women is no higher than for that of men. This argument is somewhat spurious however because the official statistics do not in any case provide us with an accurate picture of the differential involvement in crime by men and women. Any calculations about proportionate increases are therefore unlikely to be helpful. Nevertheless there remains a widespread belief that women are not only becoming more criminal but also more violent. The evidence for this, if evidence is necessary to the perpetuation of this contemporary 'moral panic', is mainly experiential. That is to say there exists a 'feeling' amongst social workers and other welfare agencies that their young female clients are more violent than they used to be (cf. Hart, 1975) and this 'experience' has been taken up by the press and elevated to the level of a significant social problem. Unfortunately the meaning of violence is rarely considered and we have little information as to which acts are so defined. It is quite possible that defiant acts by women and girls may be more readily interpreted as violent than if they were enacted by boys simply because we have different expectations of the behaviour of boys and girls. If for example we expect girls to be passive and 'feminine' then, when they are perceived by others to fail to live up to the stereotype, their actions will appear all the more shocking or threatening. Additionally we need to consider the possibility that the behaviour of female offenders may have hardly changed at all, but that the perceptions of their behaviour may have been radically affected by the belief that women are emulating the actions of men. As Smith proposes: 'It could well be argued that the recent increase in officially recorded violence among girls suggests that a change in definition, rather than in behaviour *per se*, has already taken place'

(Smith, 1975, p. 11). What is being suggested here is that the police, social workers and other agents of social control are more ready to define deviant behaviour by women and girls as violent or 'masculine' because of apparent changes in the social and economic position of women in society. Smith maintains that it is unlikely that delinquent girls are more violent, or that their involvement in fights or gangs has changed remarkably. On the contrary she suggests that, because previous researchers have never interviewed female gang members, their role in delinquency has never been recorded or revealed. It has always been assumed that girls in gangs or delinquent girls enact their deviance in terms of the typical feminine role, that is that they are sexually promiscuous, they join gangs only because their boyfriends are members and they exert a calming influence on tearaway males. Smith's argument is that this picture is a fallacy. Hence we may argue that the recent perception of changes in female delinquency is not so much indicative of actual changes in the frequency and character of female delinquency but denotes a new appraisal of the situation.

The perceived changes in female delinquency and criminality may be based on statistical fallacy, a changing consciousness on the part of researchers and social workers or on actual changes in the frequency and character of the behaviour concerned, but whatever the basis it would seem that the Women's Movement has been influential in some way. The influence of 'emancipation' is extremely complex; it affects the material being and consciousnesses of not only the women who become 'emancipated' and the men whose life-styles and consciousnesses may be transformed but also those women and men who reject the principles of liberation and yet are indirectly affected. There is considerable confusion over the meaning of emancipation and the aims of the Women's Movement. To criminologists who have studied female criminality it generally means that women are beginning to imitate men; that women are becoming more criminal and more violent, and that emancipation is therefore *per se* a regrettable state of affairs. It may be argued in contradiction to this, however, that the extension of human rights and full social and economic opportunities is not merely based on a desire to emulate men but on the advancement of social justice. Moreover emancipation is not

73

synonymous with the 'freedom' to be like a man, it refers to the ability to resist stereotyped sex roles and to reject limiting preconceptions about the inherent capabilities of the sexes. If some women seem to be emulating men it is not because of the philosophy of the Women's Movement it is primarily because there are at present only two socially acceptable identities available to individuals, the stereotypical and polarized masculine and feminine models. If one is rejected the only other 'acceptable' model available is that of the other sex, there are as yet no socially legitimate alternatives.

Changes in the behaviour of women and girls, whether criminal or not, cannot always be directly related to the influence of the Women's Movement. Social movements are themselves the outcome of economic, political and historical changes and processes, and although such movements may instigate change they are also the outcome of existing changes. It is significant that amongst some women who are scornful of the Women's Movement there exists a dissatisfaction with the social order which arises out of their inferior social position and lack of legitimate opportunities. In other words the Movement does not simply cause dissatisfactions, it is often the expression of existing and experienced injustices and inequalities. It is unlikely that advocates of the Women's Movement are to be found amongst delinquent girls and criminal women —if only because the majority of individuals who become known offenders are recruited from the working classes where there does not appear to be a strong support for the Women's Movement as such. However such women and girls may well be dissatisfied with the restrictions of the stereotypical feminine role and their limited opportunities in general but the changes in their consciousness are as likely to be caused by changing material conditions as by the principles of the Women's Movement. Those theorists who assume that a simple causal relationship exists between the Movement and increases in the rate of female criminality ignore the material and structural changes that are taking place in the lives of women and girls which are to some extent independent of demands for equality of the sexes. For example, the demand for a female labour force has arisen out of shortages of male labour during periods of national crises or during economic booms rather than out of the demands of suffragists or feminists, yet it is the consequences of women working outside the home that criminologists and other social commentators have been so critical of, maintaining that this is a result of the demands of the Women's Movement alone.

One of the few studies which attempts to analyse the relationship between female emancipation and criminality in terms of economic, political and historical processes is that of Bertrand (1973). She attempts to draw together economic, legal and political variables and to relate these to the level of women's consciousness on matters concerning sexual equality and self-determination. Unfortunately, the findings of her very ambitious study tend to be rather confused and at times ambiguous. However, she did discover that in societies where the women's consciousness of their oppression and inferior status was low, where women were confined to the traditional female role within the home (e.g. Venezuela), there was little actual crime committed by women. She also attempted to discover what relationship existed between the consciousness of women in terms of their social status and the legal and penal systems' attitude towards women. For example it seemed likely to Bertrand that where women were questioning their social status and position the legal and penal systems would reflect an equally 'liberated' perspective. However, she found that in Canada, where women are relatively 'liberated', the penal and legal systems perceived female offenders as weak and 'sick' and in need of treatment. The relationship between legal and penal policy, economic development and the consciousness of women therefore remains somewhat obscure and the value of Bertrand's study lies more in the direction it maps out than the results it has achieved. The most significant aspect of her work is the emphasis she places upon the importance of not treating emancipation as an isolated social phenomenon which exists outside an historical and social context. The current popular attempt to place the responsibility for perceived changes in the crime rate of women's emancipation represents on the surface a new phase in the traditional search to locate a monocausal factor to account for female criminality. Consequently while studies of male criminality are becoming more complex and comprehensive, the phenomenon of female criminality still tends to be reduced to a single, simple cause. With the failure of biological theories of female criminality, the consequences of emancipation for women have been advanced to provide an explanation of what is perceived as a growing social problem, namely an apparent increase in female criminality. Unfortunately this type of explanation reveals a confused and simplistic understanding of the process of emancipation, its influence upon consciousness and social institutions, and its location within and alongside other social and historical developments. Such explanations, which implicitly serve the purpose of a critique of any change in women's position, have therefore merely succeeded in providing a scientistic legitimation of women's inferior social position.

Chapter 4

Prostitution, rape and sexual politics

Within the legal system the prostitute is, almost without exception,[1] considered to be a woman. The legal definition of prostitution invariably refers to a woman selling her sexuality rather than a person of either sex selling their sexuality. Consequently prostitution has traditionally been treated as a 'female' offence. In other words prostitution, or rather soliciting for the purposes of prostitution, is a sex-specific offence because the legal definition tends to ignore the existence of male prostitution. Similarly rape is legally defined as a sex-specific offence, it being assumed, within Northern European and American cultures at least, that women cannot commit rape. Thus legally only men may commit rape, women can only be guilty of aiding and abetting rape. Rape therefore is conceived of as a 'male' offence, while prostitution is conceived of as a 'female' offence and the sex-specific nature of these offences inevitably has some bearing on cultural attitudes towards both of them. If the legal code is taken as the embodiment of cultural attitudes it would seem that, as both rape and prostitution (or more properly, solicitation) are criminal acts, both rape and prostitution are condemned. However, attitudes and even the enactment (if not the letter) of the law are more complex than this. Within the sphere of sexual morality there are double-standards in the expectations of the behaviour of men and women and these double-standards are reflected in laws and practices and attitudes towards sexual behaviour. Women are expected, within our culture, to remain pure until marriage if possible and to remain faithful to one man thereafter. The woman who fails to live up to this impossibly hard standard is to a greater or lesser extent, depending historically on fluctuations in the moral code, condemned. For men however there is a different standard; indeed in order to prove oneself a 'man' at all it is seen as necessary to engage in pre- and extra-marital sexual intercourse. Our moral code therefore restricts a woman's sexuality but encourages a man to be sexually active. It seems a contradiction therefore that offences related to prostitution, which are all non-indictable, should carry relatively little punishment (usually a fine or six months' imprisonment) while rape can result in life imprisonment and was once punishable by death or mutilation.[2] There is no contradiction however if it is considered that historically women have always been treated as the property of their fathers or husbands in legal statute. The severe penalty for rape which was (and is) not always implemented was a punishment for the defilement of another man's property rather than a form of protection for women or a recognition of women's rights over their own bodies. It is significant also that historically the rapist was not the only person who was punished for in many cases the victim also lost her life or suffered a loss of esteem and the chance to marry. Indeed it may be argued still that in contemporary rape cases the victim is on trial rather than the accused. Prostitution on the other hand has not always been treated so apparently lightly by the law[3] and it would seem that the legal penalties for soliciting for the purposes of prostitution are a reflection of the realization that it is impossible to repress prostitution rather than an indication that prostitution has become socially acceptable.

It would seem therefore that the law is not necessarily a key to social attitudes but it nevertheless has had an important influence on defining areas of study for the criminologist. Because the legal definition of prostitution excludes members of the male sex most studies of prostitution concentrate on female prostitutes, thereby implicitly accepting the double-standard of morality inherent in the legal system. The study of rape however has been largely ignored by criminologists (with the exception of Amir, 1967 and 1971; and Macdonald, 1975). There are relatively few studies within the traditional body of criminological literature concerned with examining the reasons why men commit rape, under what circumstances rape occurs and what the effects on the victim may be. Rather the accounts that exist tend to focus on the legal complexities of rape trials, the difficulty of the rules of evidence in rape cases and the problem of fully protecting the accused against false accusation.[4] However, with the revival of the Feminist Movement more analytical and less legalistic studies of rape have become available.[5]

The study of prostitution

The work of Lombroso and Ferrero (1895) has already been fully discussed and yet there is a need in this chapter to consider their study of prostitution and its place in the historical development of thought about prostitution. Earlier in discussing classical theorists I stated that Lombroso and Ferrero's theory of atavism did not achieve verification from their empirical observations of female offenders. For these theorists the prostitute was an important exception however, conforming closely to the criminal type and possessing the requisite number of retrogressive characteristics indicative of atavism. But not only was the prostitute perceived of as degenerate, for Lombroso and Ferrero prostitution *per se* represented a major sign of atavism or degeneracy. They argued tautologically that all 'primitive' women are prostitutes and consequently that to be a prostitute is to be 'primitive', that is a biological throwback to an earlier evolutionary stage. Additionally their observation that all female criminals are more virile than their non-criminal counterparts provides further confirmation for the proposition that there is a basic similarity between female criminals, in this case prostitutes, and 'savage' women, that is to say women in other cultures who were thought to be exceedingly virile and sexually immoral.

Significantly this belief in the primitiveness of the prostitute is reflected in more contemporary studies. For example, in discussing juvenile prostitution Professor Gibbens states: 'Some are mentally defective but their low intelligence seems less important than their very *primitive* outlook. They are essentially *uncivilized*; wild, quite untrained and aggressive in a *primitive* way' (T. C. N. Gibbens, 1957, p. 5). (Emphasis added.) This association between the flouting of socio-sexual mores and the state of being uncivilized or primitive contains certain interesting value-judgments which are

79

based on particular cultural assumptions. First, sexual behaviour may never be, and probably never has been, free from social constraint,[6] but both Gibbens and Lombroso *et al.* naïvely equate less restrictive, or simply different, sexual mores with uncontrolled, indiscriminate sexual behaviour. Second, these different sexual mores are associated with a low degree of 'civilization' whilst it is assumed that the repression of overt sexuality in both the nineteenth and early twentieth centuries is indicative of the real- ization of a civilized society.[7] Consequently for Gibbens and Lombroso *et al.* a perceived interest in sexual matters, particularly by women, is equated with a debasement, a degeneration from civilized standards to the level of unrepressed instinct. Implicit in this argument is the assumption that prostitutes are women who are interested in sex, who do find satisfaction in indiscriminate sexual intercourse and who are apparently over-sexed. Thus it has been argued that prostitution is a method of satisfying an inherent craving for sex rather than an outcome of economic or social conditions. Such a view of prostitution is summed up by Cecil Bishop who has stated that

No doubt many people will be shocked to learn that most prostitutes deliberately choose prostitution as their occupa- tion.... She finds that prostitution affords an easy if compara- tively small income, and that it satisfies a sex craving which grows in proportion to the extent that it is indulged (Bishop, 1931, p. 66).

In this view of prostitution the sexual behaviour of the prostitute is unfavourably compared with the supposed sexual abstinence and lack of sexual interest of upper middle-class women. Indeed it was because of the myth of the asexuality of 'respectable' women pro- pounded during the Victorian era that the prostitute appeared to suffer from an excess of virility or an abnormal sex drive. Prosti- tution is therefore seen to have its origins in some form of individual pathology which may be physiologically or psycho- logically rooted. Consequently the prostitute herself is treated as the cause of prostitution and may be justifiably punished or treated for her over-sexed condition.

This attitude towards the prostitute as a depraved or over-sexed woman has however been gradually modified and finally displaced by a more popular view that she might in fact be sexually frigid or even homosexual. It was Havelock Ellis (1936) who first cast doubt on the belief in the over-sexed nature of the prostitute. He also rejected the early economic explanations of prostitution such as those put forward by Parent-Duchatelet in the mid-nineteenth century and later materialist thinkers such as Engels (1973) or Bebel (1971) who were writing at the turn of the nineteenth century, by maintaining that there is a strong psychological factor involved in becoming a prostitute. Such beliefs were consistent with the Freudian and Neo-Freudian theories of sexuality which predominated during this era.

The Freudian explanation of promiscuous sexual behaviour relates to the Oedipal syndrome and the repression of early sexual love for the parent. Freud argued that because the early attachment to parents is frustrated by the incest taboo, subsequent sexual partners become mere surrogates because with the promiscuous person the sex instinct remains attached to its first love object. Moreover because sexual partners are mere surrogates, complete satisfaction is unobtainable and, remaining unsatisfied, the individual continually searches for new partners. Hence an endless series of substitutes is created. Consequently the promiscuous person is said to have failed to progress beyond childhood when the love object is the parent. Such a person continues into adulthood cherishing the love of former authority figures (namely parents) and is unable to transfer sexual attachment satisfactorily to another. Because the prostitute is taken to be a promiscuous individual she is considered to be still trapped into her childhood, a person who has not developed sufficiently to become a normal well-adjusted adult. Hence prostitutes can be said to have certain personality defects and prostitution or promiscuity can be regarded as a psycho-pathological reaction rather than a social phenomenon. The Freudian perspective has been developed in several ways by Rolph (1955), Gibbens (1957) and Greenwald (1958) who do not necessarily address Freud explicitly but who are nevertheless influenced by his work.

In his study of prostitution Rolph argues that although economic factors may be important enough to be classed as precipitating factors in prostitution, psychological, or rather psycho-pathological factors are also considered to be of importance in generating prostitution. He maintains that the prostitute has a need to debase the male or the father-figure as a form of revenge for an unsatisfactory or traumatic childhood. This belief in the desire to take revenge on men can also be found in Gibbens's (1957) study of juvenile prostitution. Gibbens in fact names this desire the Circe complex, that is the wish to turn men into swine. In Rolph's study however the desire to debase the sexual partner is not thought to be peculiar to the woman. He maintains that the male client has a need to debase the woman or mother-figure also and therefore the prostitute serves this purpose. Consequently a symbiotic relationship is created in which the prostitute's and the client's pathological needs are satisfied. Rolph also refers to a very high incidence of petty trickery occurring within this relationship, both on the part of the prostitute and the client, the aim of which is to exploit the temporary sexual relationship beyond its contracted limits. This, it is argued, is also suggestive of personality disorders. However, both of these symptoms, the hatred of the sex object or the concomitant distaste for the man who uses a debased object, and petty trickery can also be seen to be features of non-pathological everyday life. It is a fundamental part of our sexual mores that the 'cheap' or promiscuous woman must be used but loathed. As Greer points out

It is easy when picking a path through the wilderness of sexual *mores* to fall foul of the slough of disgust, for a shameful and compulsive activity can be pushed away by attributing all the shame and all the compulsion to the partner. The woman tempted me, and I did eat (Greer, 1970, p. 253).

Thus it is not uncommon for men to find women who are an 'easy lay' repulsive, at least after the act. Such attitudes can even be found in marriage when men become impotent because they do not wish to debase their wives whom they feel should be respected. Interestingly this loathing of the sexual partner, although perhaps more common in men because of the double-standard of morality, may also be found in women. Rolph discusses the way in which some of the prostitutes in his survey felt their clients to be morally reprehensible because so many of them were being unfaithful to their wives. As the prostitutes concerned had not taken vows of chastity and were open about their sexual activities they felt their guilt to be less than their clients. Moreover as they felt they received no sexual satisfaction from their relationships they considered their involvement to be purely economic whilst they believed their clients were driven to them by their base sexual urges. The 'compulsion' that Greer talks about may therefore be said to exist in the client, not only the prostitute, and so it also becomes appropriate for the prostitute to loathe the client. It may be that the prostitute–client relationship emphasizes this loathing and disgust for the sexual partner and it may also be that this can be termed a neurotic or unbalanced state of affairs. However, the fact that it is not peculiar to this particular contractual form of sexual intercourse indicates that culturally such feelings are common and not merely a feature of a minority of individuals who are classified as prostitutes or clients.

The reference Rolph makes to 'petty trickery' can also be said to be a feature of 'normal' social behaviour rather than being indicative of personality disorder. 'Maximizing resources' or 'striking a hard bargain' are both activities which are applauded in the worlds of business and commerce. If the prostitute's trade were categorized as a commercial activity there would be little reason to assume that such behaviour was anything other than good business sense. However, Rolph's interpretation of the behaviour of the prostitute and client is influenced by the inferential structure with which he is working. Having judged the prostitute and client to be abnormal in some way their behaviour is interpreted to support his prior assumptions. Such an outcome is perhaps not surprising given the aims of the British Social Biology Council for whom the book was written. It is stated on the frontispiece of the book that the aims of the Council are: 'To preserve and strengthen the family as the basic social unit. To encourage ... the removal of conditions conducing to promiscuity ...' (Rolph, 1955). Such aims however contain a moral judgment which is based purely upon a culturally located and an historical understanding of the family as an institution, the existence of promiscuity and of the relationship between the two. The family does not have a fixed, natural or universal form but changes according to socio-economic factors and the processes of ideological transformation. Similarly promiscuity does not exist universally; members of different cultures may act in a similar way but whether those acts are termed as promiscuous depends on their moral code. Moreover the relationship between promiscuity and the family (as both are defined in Western, advanced industrialized culture) is not necessarily one of conflict. As Davis (1971) has pointed out the flourishing existence of a class of promiscuous women (namely prostitutes) is a sign of the strength of the monogamous family. Any decline in the numbers or usage of this pariah group indicates that sexual satisfaction for men is being supplied by respectable married or unmarried women. This would of course indicate a change in the behaviour of family members, most especially the female members who may in consequence be regarded as realizing their own sexual needs and achieving both sexual and economic independence. To attempt to 'strengthen the family' in the way the Council suggests would paradoxically mean regression for women's rights and status as the despised class of the 'fallen women' would return in strength whilst 'respectable' women would be further denied sexual and social intercourse for fear of defilement. It is significant that Freud, in his discussions of promiscuity, referred to both men and women as sexually promiscuous; the contemporary usage of the derogatory term promiscuous is now however almost entirely directed at women and girls. Any attempts to deal with promiscuity therefore can be interpreted as attempts to interfere with the sexual life of women and girls and not men and boys. Such a double-standard implies that promiscuous females are unnatural and problematic while males cannot be promiscuous because their sexual drive is 'naturally' irrepressible and fairly indiscriminate. The full implications of this double-standard reveal themselves in the prosecutions of prostitutes, the treatment of rape victims and offenders and the policy of institutionalizing so-called promiscuous girls.

Like Rolph, Gibbens (1957) and Greenwald (1958) in their studies of prostitution are influenced by the Freudian perspective. Both Gibbens's and Greenwald's works are predicated on the argument that prostitutes display signs of latent or manifest homosexuality. Now the Freudian explanation of female homosexuality is derived from Freud's concept of the basic bisexuality of males and females and the resolution of the Oedipal conflict. At the Oedipal stage the female child takes her father as a love object, and identifies with her mother. If however she is rejected or some other trauma should occur to interfere with 'normal' development she will change the love object from father to mother and will identify with the father rather than the mother. Thus she will stress the masculine aspects of her bisexuality.

Gibbens's theory of the significance of unconscious or latent homosexuality in prostitution is situated squarely within this Freudian perspective. However, although he relies heavily on the proposition that prostitutes are either latently or manifestly homosexual for his analysis of prostitution, Gibbens neglects to inform the reader as to how latent homosexuality is detected or observed. In the absence of any explanation it can only be assumed that the extent to which it exists is measured entirely subjectively by the observer. This omission in Gibbens's study becomes even more significant when it is realized that out of the 400 adolescent prostitutes in his sample, only 4 were overtly homosexual. Clearly the emphasis placed by Gibbens on the significance of homosexuality has still to be justified.

The influence of Freud's work is even more evident in Gibbens's analysis of the causes of prostitution and homosexuality. He maintains that 'The background and personality of these girls varied very widely but a common feature was that the girl had a strong attachment to a father who was inadequate or unable to deserve or support such attachment' (Gibbens, 1957, p. 6). In other words the appropriate love-object failed these particular girls with the result that they became latently, if not manifestly, homosexual and in consequence searched for surrogate father-figures in a succession of lovers. Gibbens places considerable emphasis on the fact that these girls show great hostility and contempt for the male sex; however, the actual manifestation of these feelings, from which Gibbens infers their hatred, seems only to be a fear of being dominated by men and a desire to reverse the dominance relationship. That this should be interpreted as 'unnatural' or an expression of hatred is indicative of the extent to which the Freudian notions of female masochism and passivity have been embraced. The desire of a man to dominate a woman is deemed 'natural' and even an expression of love but should the desire to dominate men exist in women it is treated as a sign of their rejection of biological destiny and a symptom of some basic abnormality.

Greenwald's (1958) analysis of both promiscuity and homosexuality is similar in many respects to that of Gibbens. Of the 20 call-girls he interviewed three-quarters came from broken homes and, even where the parents stayed together, all but one prostitute said she suffered rejection by both her father and her mother. Greenwald argues that as a consequence of their unstable formative years these girls suffered from sex role confusion which manifested itself in homosexuality. Rather than maintaining that promiscuity also has its roots in childhood rejection however he maintains that a series of heterosexual relationships were sought by these girls as a way of combating their fear of homosexuality and in order to prove their 'normality'. It is significant however that these girls who had both heterosexual and homosexual relationships should be labelled homosexual or lesbians. As their heterosexual relations were not restricted to clients (i.e. purely commercial) but also took place with their male pimps it would seem more appropriate to class them as bisexual. Moreover if they are bisexual it could be argued, even in Freudian terms, that their sexuality is simply not repressed by cultural restraints and that they are merely behaving according to natural inclination rather than displaying a pathology. But this is of course highly tendentious, as indeed most statements about the normality or pathology of human sexual behaviour are. As Freud states

The unsatisfactory conclusion, however ... is that we know far too little of the biological processes constituting the essence of sexuality to be able to construct from our fragmentary information a theory adequate to the understanding alike of normal or pathological conditions (Baker Miller, 1974, p. 284).

The assumption that homosexuality or promiscuity are pathological forms of sexual behaviour, can therefore be seen as little more than moral or culturally relative judgments. It can be observed that there is a tendency in the work of the theorists considered here for the moral values informing their analyses to remain implicit. The complete neglect of any attempt to address and examine the values brought to analysis means that Rolph's, Gibbens's and Greenwald's works do little more than reinforce contemporary commonsensical understandings of the phenomenon under study.

Studies of prostitution which tend to be more sociological than psychological in orientation are not necessarily free from the above criticisms although they do manifest a development in so far as prostitution is no longer treated merely as indicative of individual pathology. For example Davis (1971) analyses prostitution in terms of its functions for society, assessing it in relation to the demand for such a service created by a particular social structure. Sociological studies of prostitution also look at economic factors although, unlike the early nineteenth-century studies, they do not posit economic factors as the only major 'cause' of prostitution. Studies like that of Parent-Duchatelet in 1857 (Bullough, 1964) consider prostitution to be the outcome of *dire* economic need. In circumstances where there is no welfare service it is perhaps reasonable to interpret prostitution as the only choice between survival and starvation. In the history of advanced and affluent industrialized societies women have been forced to become prostitutes in order to stay alive or to support their families. This was particularly the case during the industrial revolution when family ties were broken and many girls from rural backgrounds found themselves unsupported in the developing towns and cities. But dire economic need is not a part of history for all cultures and societies and although the choice between starving and prostitution may no longer be a reality for many women living in the West it is still a fact of life for others living in Third World or 'developing' countries. The tendency to reject the argument that prostitution is a consequence of extreme poverty may therefore only be relevant in advanced industrialized societies where absolute poverty is uncommon (although not unknown).

The economic explanation of prostitution in affluent societies is therefore not in terms of dire need but rather in terms of the relatively limited opportunities for women in such societies to earn a living wage, to win promotion and achieve a secure career, and to be economically independent of men. Complete economic independence remains a possibility for only a small minority of women with the consequence that a majority are not only employed in low-paid, insecure work but are also dependent on husbands, lovers and fathers or, in some cases, a paternalistic Welfare State. Given such prospects prostitution may well appear a favourable career to many women. The fact that a girl can earn more as a prostitute than in more legitimate work is frequently commented upon by sociologists and psychologists and yet the economic factor is still treated as marginal to an understanding of prostitution. Clearly economic factors do not in themselves constitute the basis of an explanation of prostitution, attention must also be given to analysis of the moral and legal code. Prostitution may be treated as an economic activity or service but it is also an activity which is subject to the tenets of the legal system. Indeed it is condemned and frequently prohibited by legal statute. Yet the act of exchanging sexual favours for economic reward is not always morally or legally reprehensible. An interesting and important example is the often quoted comparison of the activities and behaviour of a respectable wife and a prostitute. As Kinsey *et al.* point out,

If the term prostitution were to be applied to all sexual acts for which either participant received some valuable consideration, it would be impossible to draw a line between the most obvious sort of commercialized prostitution and the relationship of every husband and wife (Kinsey *et al.*, 1963, p. 595).

Interestingly similar sentiments are expressed by Engels in his study of the family. He states,

Marriage ... often turns into the crassest prostitution—sometimes on both sides, but much more generally on the part of the wife, who differs from the ordinary courtesan only in that she does not hire out her body, like a wage earner on piecework, but sells it into slavery once and for all (Engels, 1973, p. 79).

Legally and morally a wife gives her husband absolute rights over her body on signing the marriage certificate; in return the husband is bound to support his wife financially. The prostitute on the other hand takes out a series of short-lived 'contracts' with several men in return for an economic reward. The significant difference between these two activities is not so much the number of men

involved as the fact that sexual relations outside the marriage contract are still condemned in European and North American
cultures. This condemnation is not a universal fact of life however
and it should be remembered that prostitution has its origins in
religious ritual (Benjamin and Masters, 1965; Goldman, 1970) and
that brothels have been legalized in the past during eras of
toleration (Benjamin and Masters, 1965, p. 54). Moral codes and
legal statutes do not arise in isolation, they originate in a specific
structural context in which the distribution of power is significant
in determining the form and content of the moral or legal code.
Questions as to why prostitutes are predominantly female and
clients predominantly male, why the prostitute is vilified at the
same time as being thought of as socially 'useful', are not answered
simply by reference to moral or legal norms.

The most obvious but least satisfactory answers to such
questions are that male sexuality is of a different order to, and is
more urgent than, female sexuality. Henriques (1968) argues that
prostitution exists to cater for 'male incontinence' and that this in
turn has its roots in biological differentiation. This particular argument is frequently developed into a justification of a double
standard of morality for men and women. Namely, that if men
cannot control their sexual urges while women either can do so or
have no sexual urges at all, it is 'obvious' that different rules must
be developed to govern their behaviour. However, studies of male
and female sexuality (i.e. Kinsey *et al.*, 1963) indicate that female
sexuality is repressed by social mores rather than being 'naturally'
reticent or non-existent. As a result, therefore, the biological
justification for the sexual and economic exploitation of women and
the existence of a double-standard of morality is shown to be
fallacious.

Kingsley Davis (1971) offers an analysis of prostitution which
accepts the conditionability of the sexual drive and which therefore
offers a social rather than a biological explanation. He discusses
prostitution in terms of a scarcity of resources arguing that sexual
attractiveness is at a premium because it is a scarce resource while
unattractiveness is a disadvantage although it can be overcome by
economic or non-sexual means (e.g. wealth, status or property).
Thus he argues that

[T]he division of labor by sex inevitably makes women dependent to some extent on their sexual attractiveness and puts men
in control of economic means. Since the economic means are
distributed unequally between classes but female attractiveness
is not, some women of lower economic means can exploit their
attractiveness for economic gain (Davis, 1971, p. 345).

However, although Davis introduces the concept of class into his
analysis, arguing that the distribution of power is class based thus
giving the middle and upper classes advantages over the working
classes in the distribution of scarce resources, two important
fallacies pervade his work on prostitution. The first relates to his
conceptual leap from sexual attractiveness relating to either sex to
female attractiveness. He states, presumably in a reference to both
men and women, that sexual attractiveness is at a premium in
contemporary industrial society, and yet he also remarks that unattractiveness can be overcome by non-sexual means. This is
interesting but requires qualification for the ability to use non-
sexual means is dependent upon access to such means. Davis
assumes that access to such means as wealth, power and status is
dependent upon socio-economic class, he neglects altogether to
recognize the existence and significance for his analysis of the
equally important dimension of sexual differentiation. Economic
means are not freely available to women in general, being particularly limited for working-class women. Women, therefore, are
not 'inevitably ... dependent ... on their sexual attractiveness',
they become dependent on sexual attractiveness because they are
not able to be economically independent or powerful within the
existing social order. The perpetuation of this social order is not
necessarily inevitable as functionalist analyses seem to imply however, and the economic significance of female sexual attractiveness
may diminish in a less patriarchal society.

The second fallacy in Davis's argument relates to his concept of
exploitation. Davis implies that 'women of lower economic means'
are able to achieve an economic advantage by way of their 'innate'
or contrived attractiveness to men of a higher socio-economic status
and he concludes that women thereby exploit their own sexual
attractiveness. He does not consider the situation of women unable

or perhaps unwilling to use this one resource in order to find economic security, nor does he attend to the inequalities inherent in the social milieu which leaves women dependent on such a transitory and subjective attribute as attractiveness to men. Rather than describing the situation as one in which women 'exploit' their own attractiveness, it seems more appropriate to consider the ways in which women are exploited sexually because of their lack of influence in economic and political spheres and their dependence on men for economic security and survival. Davis's explanation of prostitution cannot be criticized because it is not a 'true' representation of the reality of sexual politics but it can be criticized in so far as his explanation serves to do no more than provide a legitimating gloss for the existing power structure which produces inequalities between men and women and social classes in contemporary society. In his functionalist analysis existing social relationships are not only accepted but also promoted to the status of inevitabilities with the result that alternative forms of, in particular, sexual relationships immanent as possibilities within the present social order are ignored. Hence prostitution and the commercialization of sex are for Davis inevitable constituents of social life. Davis's acceptance of the present character of sexual relationships and the inequitable treatment of the members involved can be gleaned from his remarks on the punishment of prostitutes and the immunity of their clients. Talking of the clients, Davis notes that 'To throw good citizens into jail for a vice that injures no one, would cause more social disruption than correcting the alleged crime would be worth' (Davis, 1971, p. 346). Conversely he argues that the imprisonment of the prostitute causes no social disruption as she is in any case a social outcast. His analysis is indeed correct in that men are not imprisoned for using prostitutes, although the reasons he gives (namely the importance of their contribution to economic production) are somewhat controversial, whereas the fate of prostitutes (namely fines and imprisonment) is of little significance to economic production or the power structure. We can observe therefore that Davis does not criticize the form of social organization which produces such discriminatory treatment and propagates exploitative sexual relations, rather he condones the creation of a pariah class which exists in order to satisfy the sexual needs of the socially and economically 'significant' male or the deformed or perverted male who otherwise might constitute a threat to respectable women. Simone de Beauvoir has succinctly expressed this particular view of prostitution implicit in Davis's work. She states

And it has often been remarked that the necessity exists of sacrificing one part of the female sex in order to save the other and prevent worse troubles.... The prostitute is a scapegoat; man vents his turpitude upon her, and he rejects her. Whether she is put legally under police supervision or works illegally in secret, she is in any case treated as a pariah (de Beauvoir, 1974, pp. 568–9).

Davis pays scant attention to the unjust treatment of prostitutes or the existence of discriminatory laws; for him they are merely functional, operating to ensure the continuance of existing social arrangements.

To progress beyond this functionalist explanation of prostitution an understanding of sexual 'deviation' must not be isolated from an analysis of laws and law enforcement or for that matter from a realization of the ability of the actor to select and give meaning to his or her behaviour. The early biological and psychological studies of prostitution work within the legal definition of prostitution accepting unquestioningly that prostitution is a social ill needing remedy. The motivation of the individual prostitute is seen to be pathological and meaningless except where it is treated as a symptom of a personality disturbance. Here prostitutes are seen as compulsive rather than rational actors. They are diagnosed as being driven to prostitution by predisposing factors like a broken home or a traumatic childhood experience. Less biologically or psychologically informed studies of prostitution consider the wider social issues rather than the pathology of the individual; attracting and precipitating factors such as large earnings, economic pressures or simply opportunities replace the concept of predisposing factors. In such studies prostitution constitutes a career rather than a sexual aberration. Hence prostitution, like any other career, is treated as having its own ideology, apprenticeship and opportunity structure (cf. Bryan, 1973). The prostitute is then perceived to choose prostitution as a career, her decision being based rationally on her own assessment of available alternatives rather than following neurotically or compulsively from a subconscious imperative. Although Davis's functionalist explanation rejects the pathology model of the earlier studies it neglects to consider the possibility of individual self-determination, either as a present or future reality. Furthermore the variety of possible experiences or routes leading to prostitution, the meaning of the rejection of 'normal' and legitimate sexual mores, as well as the consequences of sexual discrimination and exploitation on the powerless are all ignored by the functionalist perspective in preference for a global view of the needs of 'society' which produces an ahistorical and uncritical analysis of prostitution as inevitably 'inherent in all human society'.

Clearly the studies of prostitution discussed above do not meet even the basic requirements of a feminist perspective. The concentration on female prostitution and concomitant neglect of male prostitution or the prostitute's client, the dependence on a pathology model or a presentation of analyses which merely serve to legitimate, justify or 'naturalize' unequal social and sexual relations signify a celebration of the *status quo* rather than an attempt at a rigorous analysis oriented towards the goal of liberating people from socio-culturally located common-sense perceptions of the nature of sexual relations.

The study of rape

Rape is unique amongst offences of violence in that it has failed to arouse much interest within the discipline of criminology. As a consequence of this lack of interest there is a dearth of scientific information on rape, particularly in the UK, which is frequently compensated by an abundance of lay analysis and myth. Our understanding of rape is based upon our knowledge and experience of what might be termed 'normal' sexual relations between men and women and also by folkloric or journalistic accounts of actual rapes. From such sources we formulate opinions and understandings about rape, namely that it is a qualitatively different act to mutual and reciprocal lovemaking, and that it is an act carried out by men with sexual problems who are unable to control their sexual desires. In popular accounts rapists are portrayed as plainly distinguishable from 'normal' men particularly in that they are thought to have no alternative or legitimate sexual outlet[8] and also in their desire to humiliate and debase their victims. The stereotypical rapist is therefore thought to be a sexual psychopath, having little in common with other men. Similarly his victim is often thought to have little in common with ordinary women, it being assumed that only a foolish or reckless woman would be found in circumstances where a rape may take place or that only a sexually promiscuous woman would dress or act in a manner likely to arouse uncontrollable sexual desire.

Such popular accounts and beliefs however bear little resemblance to the findings of rape studies (cf. Amir, 1971) or the personal accounts of many rape victims (cf. Connell and Wilson, 1974). Nevertheless these myths have important consequences in particular because the cultural stereotype of the rape event often serves to define real experiences of rape as merely over-energetic sexual intercourse. In other words, if rape is perceived in the above mythical terms, acts of forcible sexual intercourse which do not fit into the prescribed pattern cannot be readily comprehended or accepted as rape. For example if the rapist is an acquaintance or friend of the victim he will not neatly fill the stereotyped picture of the rapist as a pathological stranger. On the other hand if the rapist is a married man with a family, friends and social responsibilities the isolated, sexually frustrated psychopath category will seem inappropriate. In such circumstances it becomes difficult to imagine that a rape has taken place. The stereotyped picture of the rapist therefore creates a situation in which it is difficult for a 'normal' male to imagine he could be a rapist. Similarly it is difficult for the 'normal', respectable woman to imagine that she could be raped because of the belief that rape only occurs to certain types of women. When a rape occurs therefore psychological processes may follow whereby the victim and the offender engage in interpretative work, interpreting or re-interpreting the rape event, and circumstances leading up to the event, according to their respective understandings of rape. Hence the rape can either be denied (because neither victim nor rapist fits into the stereotype categories) or the victim can redefine herself in terms of her knowledge of women who are raped, namely that she is largely responsible for her own demise. That such reinterpretation takes place would seem to be supported by the manifestation of guilt feelings in many rape victims, guilt feelings which may be concretized by the attitude of the police and courts who often appear to treat the rape victim as the responsible party in the offence (cf. Weis and Borges, 1973; Holmstrom and Burgess, 1975). Where the rape fits into the cultural stereotype, for example where the rapist is a stranger or where the victim is treated violently, it seems that the victim suffers less guilt feelings and is more likely to be treated as a victim by the legal system. The rape stereotype would therefore appear to have certain consequences for the victim, both in her psychological reaction to rape and in her treatment by the legal system. It is of the utmost importance therefore for the mythology embraced by this stereotype of rape to be exposed and to begin to achieve this we must understand the basis of our common-sense perceptions of rape.

The mythology of rape

One of the most pervasive myths which feed our distorted understanding of rape is the belief in the urgent sexual potency of men. Men are believed to have a virtually uncontrollable sexual desire, which once awakened must find satisfaction regardless of the consequences. Thus it is argued that if a woman teases or provokes a man (that is according to his interpretation of her behaviour and irrespective of her understanding of her own behaviour and intentions) he cannot be held responsible for his actions because his sexual urge is too strong to be controlled. Men are therefore deemed to be subject to an extremely strong biological imperative, to be biologically determined, at least as far as the sphere of sexuality is concerned.

The basic fallacy of the male sex-drive myth however lies in the belief that rape is a spontaneous act (an immediate response to desire) and that it is a purely sexual act engaged in for the purpose of sexual satisfaction. First, on the question of spontaneity, Amir (1971) found that in his study of rape in Philadelphia in 1958 and 1960, a total of 70 per cent of the rapes listed in police files were

95

planned. By a planned rape Amir refers to a situation in which 'the place was arranged, elaborate enticement was employed, or the victim was deliberately sought and a plan was made to coerce her into sexual relations in the place of the initial meeting, or elsewhere' (Amir, 1971, p. 141). Of the other rapes 11·4 per cent were partially planned, that is vague plans were made after meeting the victim, and 15·9 per cent were explosive, that is opportunities for sexual exploitation occurred unexpectedly. Planning is shown to be a particular feature of multiple rapes with 90 per cent of group rapes and 82·8 per cent of pair rapes being planned while 58·4 per cent of single rapes were planned. The Philadelphia study therefore tends to negate the belief in the relationship between the urgent needs of male sexuality and rape, at least as far as reported rapes are concerned.

Second, the belief that rape is a method of gaining sexual satisfaction seems doubtful when the degree of violence and degradation inflicted on the victim is considered. Again using data from six hundred and forty-six cases in Amir's study, it was found that force of some kind was used in 85·1 per cent of the cases. Beating occurred in 45 per cent of the cases, choking in 11·5 per cent and roughness in 28·5 per cent. Intimidation with a weapon which is classed by Amir as 'non-physical' force occurred in 21·1 per cent of the cases. Sexual humiliation in addition to forced intercourse occurred in 26·8 per cent of the rape cases, repeated intercourse being the most common form (42·8 per cent) and fellatio the next most common (34·7 per cent). Unless we can accept that sexual need and desire are only to be fulfilled when accompanied by alarming degrees of violence and sexual degradation, it must be the case that rape is an act of extreme hostility and not a purely sexual act. As Greer argues

It is a vain delusion that rape is the expression of uncontrollable desire or some kind of compulsive response to overwhelming attraction. Any girl who has been bashed and raped can tell how ludicrous it is when she pleads for a reason and her assailant replies, 'Because I love you' or 'Because you're so beautiful' or some such rubbish. The act is one of murderous aggression, spawned in self-loathing and enacted upon the hated other (Greer, 1970, p. 251).

Rape is a violent expression of hatred for women, not of sexual desire for them. Which is not to argue that men do not achieve some kind of physical pleasure from raping women, although as Herschberger (1970) indicates this pleasure is so one-sided that rape is really a form of 'intravaginal masturbation'; the woman is merely the object which contains the means to sensory stimulation.

There is of course a serious methodological problem involved in making assumptions about rapists and rape victims when the available data stem from rape events that have been reported to the police or from imprisoned rapists. Rape is well known as an offence which is grossly under-reported and so it is unlikely that known rapes or rapists will be representative of rapes or rapists in general. It is also likely that the class bias found in police and court statistics which apply to other types of offences, applies to rape also. Weis and Borges (1973) argue that the trauma of rape is so great that the victim will not willingly describe the event to strangers and officials. Significantly they maintain that middle-class victims of rape are more likely to go to psychiatrists, gynaecologists or private hospitals where they can be assured secrecy, while less fortunate rape victims go to public hospitals where there is a policy of informing the police of suspected rape cases. Hence the police are likely to have a disproportionate amount of information on rapes occurring in poor areas. This in turn is likely to lead to a disproportionate number of working-class Blacks and Whites being charged with rape, giving the impression that rape is an offence of a working-class nature. Of course the class and living area of the victim does not always mean her assailant is of the same class or from the same area although Amir does show that there is a fairly strong similarity between the socio-economic background of the victim and rapist and that there is a strong likelihood they will come from the same area or district. (Only 2·7 per cent of rape victims in the Philadelphia study did not live in the same area as the offender or the area where the offence took place.)

Another addition to rape mythology is the belief in female masochism. Central to this particular myth is the idea that women achieve enjoyment from masochistic experiences, ranging, for

97

example, from a longing to be raped to taking pleasure in pain and humiliation. Rape studies which take a psychological orientation have tended to perceive rape as an individual or dyadic phenomenon rather than a social one in which rape rates can be related to a particular culture or general attitude towards women. Consequently concentration has been focused entirely on either the victim or the offender in order to discern why particular types of people are involved in sexual offences rather than any attempt being made to discover how social factors produce rapists and victims. The belief in female masochism stems from psychoanalytic theories of female sexuality which assume there is a direct relationship between the female biology and masochism (cf. Horney, 1974). Whether the relationship between masochism and female sexuality is biologically determined or a consequence of socialization is an important question which, however, cannot be considered here. Nevertheless it must be noted that one implication of the biological determinist position is the assumption that all women are 'naturally' masochistic, an assumption that clearly cannot be substantiated. Whether some women (or more women than men) have masochistic fantasies is not at issue here; although we may note in passing that people rarely attempt to act out their fantasies and furthermore that in rape fantasies the victim is often in the position of selecting a 'rapist' she finds desirable—this is clearly not the case in reality. The importance of the belief in masochism is that rape comes to be thought of as pleasurable for the victim, rape thereby becoming virtually a victimless crime.

There are cultural and physiological aspects to the belief that women enjoy being raped. First, there is the cultural aspect. In a society where women are allowed sexual enjoyment only within very strict limits and where all the shame and responsibility for sex lies on their shoulders, it is often assumed that it is a massive relief to be 'taken' by force as this can absolve all guilt and rape can be a purely context-free sensual experience. This account however overlooks that in such a society women not only live by the rules of their culture, they actually believe in them, such that illicit sex of any kind is still a shameful and repugnant experience for them. They are not magically removed from their social context; on the contrary that context serves to punish them further. It might be argued, however, that in contemporary industrial society women do not experience such traditional cultural restraints any longer and that rape for the modern sexually 'liberated' woman is merely one more experience, an epitome of the sexual pleasure without social ties or restrictions with which she is well acquainted. This point of view totally overlooks the fact that any form of liberation involves an increase in self-determination and freedom of choice and it is precisely these existential states to which rape represents the complete antithesis. Rape for the sexually 'liberated' or 'unliberated' women is a traumatic experience and for neither is it an opportunity for abandoned sensual pleasure. Second, the physiological aspect of the belief that women enjoy rape is based on a belief that stimulation to the erogenous zones will automatically and unavoidably lead to pleasurable sensations. Thus a stimulus-response model of sexual responsiveness is created and any other considerations, such as disgust for the stimulator, fear or shame, are not considered to be variables which interfere with our motor responses. However, as Herschberger argues, 'The actual result of forced stimulation can be anaesthesia or intense pain. This is true of the male if the stimulus is resisted or unwelcome. Yet the assumption that women are totally receptive has given rise to the belief that a rape victim cannot avoid feeling pleasure' (Herschberger, 1970, p. 24). The contexts in which sexual contact takes place, whether the partner is chosen or not, whether 'loved' or not, all serve to make that contact either pleasurable or intensely painful. Sensory nerves do not act in isolation from cognition and what may be delightful to our senses in one context may disgust us in another. This assumption that the victim does receive some pleasure from such an assault reduces the victim's rights to protection by the law because the crime then becomes virtually victimless and victimless crimes are rarely thought of as being of a serious nature since no victims requiring protection are created.

Closely linked with the psychoanalytically based belief in female masochism is the more sociologically oriented concept of victim precipitation in the rape context. The work of Amir (1971) has placed particular emphasis on those relationships between the rapist and the victim which can be interpreted as precipitating the rape. Amir discusses the rapist-as-stranger myth in his study of rape in Philadelphia, pointing out that rapist and victim are frequently known to each other, if only by sight, and he also shows that rapes take place most frequently within the 'participant's' place of residence, involving a considerable degree of planning. He therefore largely dismisses the stereotypical concept of rape, treating rape as an interaction situation in which two parties are involved, both of whom have some influence over the outcome of the situation. Amir stresses the importance of the interpretation of the Other's actions, significantly pointing out that the nature of that action is not as important as the meaning or interpretation the Other gives to that action. He states, 'Victim behaviour can be outright and overt seduction, but whether it is really so is not very important. What is important is the offender's interpretation of her actions within the then current situation' (Amir, 1967, p. 493). Amir allows therefore that reasonable behaviour on the part of a woman may still be interpreted as provocative by the rapist and clothing which is mundane to most may 'invite' the man for whom it signifies something special. But victim precipitation in Amir's terms does not merely refer to the situation in which the rapist misinterprets social cues and the victim is the unwitting cause of precipitating the rape. He states, 'If the victim is not solely responsible for what becomes the unfortunate event, at least she is often a complementary partner' (Amir, 1967, p. 493). In other words Amir maintains that the victim must bear the responsibility of the rapist's (mis)interpretation of her actions because any behaviour which is contrary to social expectations about appropriate female behaviour is open to (mis)interpretation. Thus if a woman does not reject a man's advances strongly enough, if she rejects him after he believes he is likely to succeed or if she uses indecent language she is actively responsible for precipitating the impending rape. Unfortunately, as Weis and Borges (1973) have pointed out, this concept of victim-precipitation is virtually synonymous with 'blaming' the victim for her fate.

Victim precipitation assumes that men and women internalize and operate with the same set of interpretative rules as far as sexual relationships are concerned. Yet men are encouraged to be assertive, women relate sex with love or some ultimate goal while men can treat it as a goal in itself. The meaning of a sexual encounter is likely to be very different for men and women therefore, for while she is sensitized to cues relating to romance or relationships (including platonic) he is sensitized to cues which imply sexual intercourse. This relates particularly strongly to the point Amir makes about the rape victim's failure to repel a man's advances strongly enough. In the pre-rape situation the woman's response is geared to her own expectations of the relationship not to the man's expectations; a moderate rejection of a sexual advance would therefore seem reasonable. On the other hand, for the man whose aim is intercourse the gentle rebuff can be interpreted as a form of subtle encouragement, a response conforming to his expectations of her reaction to his advance, namely that she will require 'persuasion' or will seem unwilling because either she lacks a strong sexual instinct or is responding according to the moral requirements of what is expected of women. It should be remembered also that women are not encouraged to deflate men's egos (if they do they become 'castrating') and what is more they rarely possess the means (i.e. credibility, courage or strength) either to convince men of their actual intentions, such that misinterpretation is not possible, or to repel a man's advances should reason fail. As Weis and Borges have pointed out, women will rarely make a scene if they are molested in crowded trains or buses. They continue:

Such actions, however, contain for both parties elements of foreplay to rape. By not protesting, the woman opens herself to a social dilemma. She appears to be consenting to his 'invitation', and thus precluding the definition of his action as sexual advances without consent (Weis and Borges, 1973, p. 83).

Often when the intention of the would-be rapist is clear to the victim she cannot respond in a defensive way as she is immobilized with fear. Moreover if she knows the rapist (Amir found that participants were known to each other in 48 per cent of the Philadelphia cases) 'her emotional investment in the person ... will make any definition, other than rape more plausible and acceptable to her' (Weis and Borges, 1973, p. 83). The victim therefore postpones her reaction and the rapist can either (mis)interpret this as consent or can merely use it to his advantage in securing his goal. After the event the rapist's interpretation of the woman's behaviour is likely to remain the same. For the woman however a process of re-interpretation and reflection is likely to occur in which she will begin to realize that her expectations and original interpretations were not compatible with those of her attacker. One possible consequence of this process is that she may believe she reacted stupidly and will therefore feel herself to be largely responsible for her assault.

The mistake of psychological and psychoanalytical approaches to rape and rape victims is that they perceive each event in terms of the idiosyncrasies and problems of the individual, thus tacitly accepting the social context which creates a situation in which all women are potential legitimate rape victims. This particular mistake does not appear in Amir's work. However although he advances the study of rape, in particular by pointing to the cultural and subcultural influences which create rapists, he fails to give sufficient consideration to the social context of the victim. Rather she is treated as bringing her fate upon herself in an individualistic fashion. His commitment to an interactionist analysis is therefore rather one-sided and his work, which is a leading study in the area of rape, does little to clarify our understanding of the rape victim and, consequently, little to clarify our understanding of rape as a whole.

In fact neither rape nor prostitution can be understood in isolation from an analysis of the position of women and the attendant sexual mores operating within a given culture. In cases of rape the accused may frequently claim that the victim's 'No' meant 'Yes', in cases of seduction the woman's 'No' may ultimately have become 'Yes'. We cannot assume from this however that women do not know what they want. On the contrary we must understand the game that women are obliged to play and the circumstances in which we participate, namely from a predominantly vulnerable position with only one valued asset, basically sexual availability. Traditionally women have used their sexual attractiveness for an ulterior purpose, either social mobility, marriage or economic security (or all three). As Davis succinctly puts it:

Formerly ... a respectable woman gave her sexual favours only in return for the promise of a stable relationship and economic support.... The girl could thus use her relatively short period of maximum attractiveness to settle her future in the best way possible—by marriage. This is still the bargain that many girls in contemporary society would like to make, and some of them do; but their bargaining position has been undermined by the growing loss of family and community controls (Davis, 1971, p. 334).

Women, then, have used their sexuality to bargain, traditionally they have had little else to bargain with, but inevitably they have been called sly, mercenary or 'prick teasers' because of it. Modern women have therefore inherited a tradition of sexual bargaining and a role of sexual mercenary. This in turn means that women's attitudes and feelings towards sexual intimacy are assumed by men to be ambiguous because it was generally accepted that respectable women would not give up their virginity without a struggle. Moreover perseverance and success for the man frequently entailed engagement and marriage, thus an exchange of commodities took place and the woman's sexuality (and often virginity) was exchanged for economic security to be provided by the man. However, as Davis points out, the situation facing contemporary women is quite different. Her bargaining power is reduced because her honour is no longer protected by her family and the legal system as it was when a daughter was defined as her father's property. In such circumstances the man is not obliged to exchange anything for his sexual satisfaction and perseverance, when a woman rejects his sexual advances, may become rape rather than marriage. This reduction of female sexuality to a market commodity in everyday life is also clearly emphasized in the prostitute-client relationship; the prostitute's accomplishment of numerous bargains each day confirming the value that is placed on female sexuality as a commodity.

The relationship between prostitution, rape and everyday sexual politics goes beyond the commodity status of female sexuality however. In many relationships outside prostitution and rape 'the female ... permit(s) herself to be used when she is not sexually interested or at most mildly aroused (and) finds herself in the midst of an unsatisfactory experience' (Thompson, 1974). The question is why this should happen and also why men should apparently be able to demand sexual satisfaction whenever they desire it. Clearly this is related to the beliefs already discussed above which maintain that the male sex drive is urgent and irrepressible while the female is largely dormant. But this is only a partial explanation for we must also understand the existing power structure between men and women that has sanctioned the repression of female sexuality and the amplification of male sexuality. The property status of women and the archaic laws which still bind her to a subordinate status[9] uphold the notion that female sexuality can be contained while male sexual urges cannot. It is a belief that is adhered to as much by women as by men, with the consequence that prostitutes and rape victims are frequently stigmatized while the client and the rapist are 'understood'. The relationship between sex and violence is also largely a consequence of the nature of sexual politics in which men have legitimate authority and women have no power or ability to defend themselves. Culturally men are expected to be aggressive and dominant in all spheres of action so it is hardly surprising that in sexual relations similar expectations prevail. In fact the connection between male sexuality and aggression has been legitimated by psychologists and the legal system alike. An example of the former is Wilson's position, which is expressive of the psychological tradition. He maintains, 'The male sex drive is basically a need to dominate, so that rape and sadism are not truly "sexual" deviations' (Wilson, 1974, p. 133). Whilst in the latter case an example of the legal legitimation of aggressive male sexuality is the law which allows a husband to rape or sexually assault his wife. Typical of the judiciary's attitude towards male and female sexual relations is Lord Dunedin's statement:

If the wife is adamant in her refusal the husband must choose between letting his wife's will prevail, thus wrecking the marriage, and acting without her consent. It would be *intolerable* if he *were to be conditioned in his course of action by the threat of criminal proceedings.*
[Footnote] It is indeed permissible to wish that some *gentle*

violence had been employed (Smith and Hogan, 1973, p. 325). (Emphasis added.)

It is therefore socially and legally acceptable that men should use aggression and violence for sexual ends. As Weis and Borges (1973) have pointed out, the ordinary rapist, unlike other sexual offenders such as child molesters or child rapists, 'ranks high in the male prison hierarchy', thus indicating an apparent approval of violent sexual encounters. While Griffin (1971) points out that convicted rapists differ from the 'normal' sexual personality only by having a greater tendency to express violence and rage.

Rapists may then be said to be 'normal' given a social context in which male sexuality and aggression are equated and female sexuality is repressed and rendered passive. Rape must therefore be understood in terms of male and female sex roles in a given culture in a specific socio-historical context. Individualistic explanations of rape which imply that rape is symptomatic of personality disorders (i.e. a fear of castration, a sexual perversion or female masochism) ignore totally the social context in which rape occurs. Similarly prostitution must be understood in terms of a culture in which the bargaining of sexual favours is an integral part of everyday life and in fact the traditional basis of marriage. However to establish the basic interconnection between prosti-tution, rape and 'normal' sexual relations (i.e. voluntaristic and not for immediate tangible gain) is not to completely collapse the distinctions which remain between these social phemonena. In her paper entitled 'Female deviance and the female sex role' (1975), K. Rosenblum argues that the distinction between the non-deviant woman and the prostitute can be made not in terms of moral judg-ments or the bargaining of sex but in terms of primary and secondary deviation. She maintains that the female sex role con-tains elements of primary deviation in that women in general do exchange sexual favours for a reward of some kind. However, she states: 'The non-deviant woman, regardless of the degree of prosti-tution implicit in her role, does not undergo the emotional and physical damage experienced by prostitutes' (Rosenblum, 1975, p. 183). The prostitute differs from the non-deviant woman because she has progressed beyond the stage of primary deviation to secondary deviation. At the primary deviation stage societal reaction attempts to 'normalize' the deviant behaviour which may be to remind the deviant of normative expectations or to ignore the event. However, if the deviant persists and the deviance becomes increasingly visible the behaviour may be labelled as deviant. Prior to his labelling process the deviant goes through a process of what Lemert (1967) calls 'valuation' in which the rewards of 'normalizing' or continuing a deviant career are compared. Once the deviant has decided to continue the deviant career stigmatization and punishment follow and the deviant's life-style is obliged to change to accommodate such eventualities. Thus the prostitute must live a fairly secret life which is organized around attracting clients but avoiding the police, arrest and other hazards. These contingencies are not a part of the non-deviant woman's life and so her life-style remains 'normal' and socially acceptable.

It may also be feasible to distinguish between rape and 'normal' sex in terms of primary and secondary deviance. In the way that the female sex role may be said to embrace primary deviance in terms of sexual bargaining so the male sex role may similarly embrace primary deviance in terms of aggressive or violent sexuality. From the perspective of the woman involved, an experience of primary deviation in her chosen sexual partner may be quite acceptable while the trauma of a rape situation involving secondary deviation will undoubtedly be extremely damaging and stigmatizing. For the man the progression from primary to secondary deviation is however likely to be less traumatic and damaging than for the rape victim (or for the prostitute in her deviant career). Unlike the process of valuation through which most committed deviants are thought to progress, for the rapist the evaluation of legitimate and illegitimate values may not be so explicit. Becoming a rapist does not necessarily involve a dramatic change in life-style,[10] or values, because rape is still perceived as an explosive, isolated event. As rape cannot be seen to have a career structure with some notion of a continuing commitment and specific ideology to sustain it like other forms of deviance or crime, there is no concomitant requirement for an underground existence or special contacts and rituals. With the exception of some politically and ideologically motivated rapists,[11] the rapist bears a strong resemblance to the white-collar criminal who shares the same values as his non-criminal colleagues, with regard to sex and business respectively. Both may even boast about their achievements and are only stigmatized or labelled deviant at the stage of arrest by the police and appearance in court. The primary and secondary deviation distinction introduced by Rosenblum is therefore valuable to the extent that it allows us to distinguish between prostitution, rape and socially acceptable sexual behaviour, but its appropriateness is limited to the social consequences of deviancy for women rather than men. It cannot account for the fact that sexual deviance in women is more highly stigmatized than in men, nor can it account for why agencies of social control appear to be more concerned with 'normalizing' sexual deviance in women than man.

Conclusion

In this chapter I have been concerned to show the presence and acceptance of culturally based, common-sense understandings of prostitution and rape in traditional criminological theories and perspectives. In general such studies have tended to be either too biologically or too psychologically oriented, employing a highly deterministic model of human nature. Consequently they have inclined towards the assumption that rape and prostitution are aberrations within social behaviour and symptomatic of individual pathology. They have overlooked the way in which both of these forms of sexual *deviation* may be interpreted as mere extensions of cultural attitudes towards sexuality in general and women in particular. In fact the subordinate position of women in contemporary industrial society is rarely addressed and never satisfactorily analysed in such studies, it being assumed that sexual stratification is a reflection of the natural order of things. This is somewhat surprising when it is considered that sexual differentiation and exploitation are the basis of both prostitution and rape.

Chapter 5

The treatment of female offenders

Social theory is frequently conceived to be an abstract activity which is independent and remote from the social world it attempts to understand and explain. Consequently theoretical work is rarely considered in terms of its effect upon the social phenomenon under investigation although a minority of social theorists have drawn attention to the dialectical relationship between theory and the social world. The majority of social scientists still appear to be convinced of their status as detached observers of social phenomena and, as a result, remain unable to recognize the moral, political and practical implications of their theoretical work. This state of affairs within criminology in particular has meant that little, if any, work has addressed the question of the relationship between social theories of female criminality, everyday conceptions of the female offender, social policy and the treatment of offenders. This is in spite of the fact that criminology has traditionally been aligned with penal and social policy-making institutions, the most important in the UK being the Home Office. Criminology's major function has been the study and explanation of different forms of criminality and the evaluation of the effectivity of various types of treatment and punishment. Hence the established criminologist has traditionally been inclined to be in the position of consultant to official institutions on matters of penal policy and therefore directly influential where policy is concerned. Now as far as the influence of theories of female criminality upon everyday conceptions of the female offender and penal policy is concerned there is little evidence to suggest such a direct or overt relationship. However, there are grounds for arguing that a relationship does exist and that current theories do influence both attitudes towards female offenders in general and policy decisions in particular.

The process by which social theories may influence or modify our comprehension of, and attitudes towards, female offenders is not self-evident. In discussing the way in which sociological theories enter into everyday consciousness Allen describes one way in which this relationship can be manifested. He states:

Theories enter into the ideological process and emerge in an abbreviated, often vulgarized, sloganized form embedded in language and thought processes alike. They form the basis of common-sense attitudes. They are transmitted through the family, enter into folklore, get expression through the educational system and are monotonously repeated through the mass media. In a variety of subtle ways conventional theoretical explanations enter the consciousness of individuals and provide them with instant explanations (Allen, 1974, p. 10).

Consequently, in spite of appearing abstract and remote, theoretical explanations can exert an influence upon everyday life and the consciousness of all members of a society (including offenders, social workers, police officers and policy makers) will be influenced by the communication of such ideas.

An interesting account of the process by which theoretical explanations become a part of our shared understanding of social phenomena can be gleaned from Cressey's (1971) discussion of kleptomania. Cressey, in his paper on differential association, role theory and compulsive crimes, considers the influence of linguistic constructs on social behaviour. In particular he considers how linguistic constructs affect the way in which the individual interprets his or her own behaviour and the understanding he or she brings to social encounters. Thus Cressey argues that once a term like kleptomania, which was originally an abstract and obscure psychological concept, has become a part of the conceptual currency of everyday life, it has an influence over cognitive processes and ultimately modifies behaviour, or at least the interpretation of that behaviour. Cressey's argument hinges on a belief that the source of motivation is social rather than biological and that language and vocabulary transmit this motivation. In other words language defines the parameters of our knowledge through cognitive processes (whether rational or irrational) rather than being impelled by unaccountable biological forces.

When an offender is unable to offer a seemingly rational or reasonable account of her motivation it may appear that rational motivation is absent and that action is produced by forces beyond the control of the offender. But the lack of an account, or the lack of an account which is acceptable to social control agencies, does not mean that there is an absence of social motivation. For example, were an offender to rely on vague concepts of impulse or uncontrollable urges to explain a particular form of behaviour it would not necessarily mean that the offender was driven by such forces. On the contrary the offender might only be relying on an explanation or excuse that will reduce her culpability. However, it is also possible that an offender is not disguising the 'real' reason for an offence (e.g. shoplifting) when she offers explanations in terms of uncontrollable urges simply in order to escape prosecution or punishment. It is also possible that she is unable to offer herself a reasoned account for her behaviour. Significantly it is usually only with deviant or criminal behaviour that we are required to supply a reasonable or rational explanation for our behaviour, conformity rarely requires justification. This is because the reasons for conformity are assumed to be shared by all members of society while non-conformist behaviour is not immediately understandable or acceptable to others. Yet in either a conformist or deviant situation a considered rational explanation may be difficult to accomplish and the actor may frequently make use of accounts or explanations that are socially approved and acceptable rather than individually valid or meaningful. The consequence of resorting to such accounts are more important in the case of deviant or criminal behaviour however. This is because the failure to give an adequate account, or the tendency to rely on impulse or psychological or biological urges as explanations, results in a confirmation of the belief that deviants are 'sick' or lack the ability to control their own actions. The shoplifter who claims that she has no use for the stolen goods and that she cannot understand why she stole is conforming to the stereotype of the kleptomaniac. She is not necessarily deliberately trying to 'pass' as a kleptomaniac in order to avoid punishment, although this may happen, rather she may be unable to provide herself with an 'adequate' explanation let alone verbalize one to the authorities. Moreover part of the motivation to theft in the first place, besides need or desire for the object(s) concerned, may have been a belief, based upon a knowledge of kleptomania, that some acts of theft are not the full responsibility of the actor and are therefore less reprehensible. In her study of shoplifting in Holloway Dr Epps (1962) found that the most common explanation of theft conformed to the kleptomaniac image. She states:

> The degree of premeditation was hard to assess. . . . It was rarely allowed that anything more than a sudden impulse preceded the act. . . . The phrase 'of no use to me' became a familiar one in the course of excuses and explanations for the theft (Epps, 1962, pp. 132–3).

A possible consequence of the recourse to available pseudo-psychological accounts or explanations in cases like this is not only that the offender may come to (re)define her behaviour as independent of her own control but that the authorities will also do so and thus treat such offenders as 'sick' individuals rather than rational beings. It is possible therefore that where sociological or psychological theories enter our 'language and thought processes' in a modified form and we use them as instant explanations and acceptable accounts of our behaviour, we reinforce certain attitudes towards, and understandings of, our behaviour.

In advanced industrialized societies there tends to be an *a priori* assumption that women are irrational, compulsive and slightly neurotic. Criminological theories of female criminality have reflected this predominant paradigm, often using unfounded assumptions about the 'true' nature of women as proof of their assertions and explanations of female behaviour. In turn such theories have influenced general conceptions of the female offender and possibly the offender's perception of herself or at least the type of accounts she may offer as explanation of her behaviour. This may then serve as a reinforcement of existing *a priori* assumptions about the nature of female criminality. Such theories may therefore be influential in modifying common-sense perceptions of female offenders or they may merely reinforce existing attitudes and comprehensions; in either case the influence of theories of female criminality is of a potentially political and practical nature requiring consideration and examination in all areas of the treatment of female offenders by the legal and penal systems.

Women and the criminal law

The criminal law is generally held to be equally applicable to both sexes regardless of the type of offence involved. For example it is stated that

The criminal law applies equally to women as to men and provides in general the same range of penalties for the same offences irrespective of the sex and marital status of the offender and affords the same protections to the accused (Central Office of Information Reference Pamphlet 67, 1975, p. 7).

This official statement is somewhat misleading however because in practice both sex and marital status may affect the legal definition of an offence, the assessment of culpability and the protection of both the accused and the victims of criminal offences. For example, a woman may not be charged with the offence of rape although she may be guilty of aiding and abetting such an act (Halsbury's Statutes of England, 1969). Similarly only a woman can be convicted of infanticide because the definition of this offence relates primarily to the biological function of giving birth. In one special case both the sex and marital status of the offender is significant in terms of culpability, namely where a married woman commits an offence in the presence of her husband. In this case the law recognizes that the woman may have been following her husband's instructions and, with the exception of cases of murder and treason, allows her a special defence plea. This legal anomaly is based on the idea that husbands occupy a position of authority over their wives while wives dutifully obey their husbands, and although it may act as a form of discrimination in favour of married women it is founded upon the legal recognition of a woman's inferior social status in society. However, like other legal anomalies which are based on traditional paternalistic and chauvinistic attitudes towards women, this exception in the law is likely to be removed or to fall into disuse as the position of women in society improves.

In some respects it appears that the law is favourably inclined towards female offenders (this is the most commonly held conception of the treatment of women in law), but there are equally situations in which the law discriminates against women. For example the Street Offences Act (1959) discriminates against women who are prostitutes while exonerating men who use prostitutes or solicit women. Alternatively the law on rape does not provide women with sufficient protection against such an assault although in non-sexual offences women appear to have equal rights and protection as men. I shall examine these two examples of discrimination in detail.

Prostitution

The current law on prostitution was devised by the Report of the Committee on Homosexual Offences and Prostitution in 1957. This Committee, which is better known as the Wolfenden Committee, was given the task of formulating measures which would prevent prostitution from continuing to be a public nuisance. Until the time when the recommendations of this Committee were implemented, prostitutes had been allowed to solicit custom openly on the streets and in order for a police officer to charge a woman with soliciting it required a witness to give evidence that the woman had caused 'annoyance' to passers-by. Understandably few people were willing to involve themselves in court proceedings simply because they had been temporarily annoyed and so prostitution flourished openly. It was the public nature of prostitution however that caused the government to act because it was felt that the sight of prostitutes in the streets was generally offensive. The Wolfenden Committee was therefore given the task of finding means to remove prostitutes from public notice rather than to abolish prostitution. The Committee achieved this goal by strengthening the police powers of arrest for soliciting. The law now no longer requires evidence of 'annoyance' to passers-by and in addition the

Committee recommended the establishment of a system of cautioning which is informally adhered to although it is not a legal requirement. The cautioning system suggests that a police officer officially cautions, on three occasions, a woman believed to be soliciting before she is arrested for such an offence. The labelling or definition of a woman as a prostitute is therefore left very much to police discretion although a minor safeguard does exist in so far as a woman who is able to show that she was mistakenly cautioned may apply to a court to have the caution removed from the official records. Once a woman has actually been arrested for soliciting she becomes known as a 'common prostitute' and if she is found soliciting again, or merely loitering in a public place, she is subject to further arrests. The present law states that 'It shall be an offence for a common prostitute to loiter or solicit in a street or public place for the purpose of prostitution' (Street Offences Act 1959, Section One, Halsbury's Statutes of England, 1969). The penalty for the first conviction for soliciting is a fine of up to £10; for the second offence it is a fine of up to £25, and for subsequent convictions it is a fine of up to £25 or up to three months' imprisonment or both. Under the present law therefore a woman becomes very vulnerable to repeated arrest once she has been labelled as a 'common prostitute'. If she is unable to solicit custom other than in public she is very likely to receive a prison sentence at some stage, or even repeatedly, during her career. Once labelled a 'common prostitute' a woman's defence against unjust arrest and conviction is drastically reduced. In effect if she denies a charge of soliciting in court it becomes a case of a police officer's word against that of a 'known' prostitute. In this situation few prostitutes attempt to defend themselves even though they may not have been 'on business' at the time of arrest (cf. Dell, 1971, ch. 4). 'Known' prostitutes therefore find they have serious restrictions placed on their social life outside of business hours. It is virtually impossible for them to live with a man or even another woman as it is immediately assumed that such people are living off immoral earnings, thereby making themselves vulnerable to a criminal charge. Also, the legal definition of a brothel, as a dwelling containing two or more prostitutes, makes it difficult for two women to live together even where only one is a prostitute.

The question of whether sexual discrimination against women is embodied in the existing legislation on prostitution has been the concern of an official Working Party set up to consider the effectiveness of the 1959 Act. Critics of the 1959 Act have argued that because only women are punished for prostitution while the solicitation of women by men is ignored by the law, a double-standard of morality exists for men and women. The Working Party have replied to this criticism with a curiously circular explanation of the law. They state,

It has ... been suggested that to define an offence by reference to the category of persons who commit it, where the same act might be committed with impunity by others, is a legal impro-priety. But this is a matter of opinion. The conduct with which the law seeks to deal is conduct which people find offensive precisely because it is committed by prostitutes in pursuing their calling; ... (Working Party on Vagrancy and Street Offences Working Paper, 1974, p. 74).

The Working Party did not reflect upon why 'people' find it offensive to witness sexual solicitation by a woman and not offen-sive where a man is concerned. The very attitude which they adopt so uncritically is a clear manifestation of the double-standard of morality, it being permissible for men to be sexually active yet reprehensible if women display similar behaviour. In effect the Working Party defends the embodiment of a sexually discrimi-natory law by reference to an equally discriminatory double-standard inherent in common attitudes.

However, the Working Party's report does at least recognize the growing menace of 'kerb-crawling'. Whereas the Wolfenden Com-mittee recognized this nuisance to 'respectable' women but did not attempt to make such behaviour unlawful because it was felt that too many respectable men would be at risk from arrest, the recent Working Party does offer practical proposals for legislation against 'kerb crawling' or related behaviour. The offence that the Working Party envisages is along the following lines:

a man persistently accosting a woman or women for sexual purposes in a street or public place in such circumstances as are likely to cause annoyance to the woman or annoyance to the public, such as residents and users of the street (Working Party on Vagrancy and Street Offences Working Paper, 1974, p. 87).

A decision as to whether an 'annoyance' had occurred would be at the discretion of the police who would be given powers of arrest where necessary. However, although such an offender would be subject to arrest and ultimately to a fine and possible imprisonment if these recommendations became law, the Working Party does not envisage a system of stigmatization and labelling for the man who solicits in this way. Thus, although the woman who solicits would still be liable to be labelled a 'common prostitute', there would be no such equivalent term for men nor concomitant loss of rights and vulnerability to further arrests and convictions. Indeed the recommendation of the retention of the term 'common prostitute' by the Working Party allows for an anomalous situation in law to be perpetuated. Once a woman is labelled a 'common prostitute' the police are able to cite her previous record in court in order to establish a fresh offence of soliciting. In practice therefore the police do not have to prove that an offender was soliciting on a specific occasion once she has become identified as a known prostitute. This makes the arrest of prostitutes a very simple process for the police, a conviction for each charge of soliciting involving a 'common prostitute' being a mere formality. In a sense therefore prostitutes are both arrested and convicted by the police because police discretion is the basis of the operation of the Street Offences Act. This renders prostitutes a very powerless section of the community, having fewer rights to protection from the law than ordinary citizens.

The Working Party, whose membership of thirteen included seven members from the Home Office and four from the police force, did not examine the nature of police discretion in its review of the law on street offences. Indeed where reference is made to police activity no consideration is given at all to possible injustices arising from the powers of discretion allowed to the police force. They state that,

[T]he evidence we have had from the police persuades us that in practice officers on street offence duties are well able to distinguish the prostitute from the respectable woman, and a caution is most unlikely to be given unless it is abundantly clear that the woman is in fact loitering or soliciting for the purpose of prostitution (op. cit., 1974, p. 79).

The criteria employed by the police for distinguishing between the prostitute and the 'respectable' woman are not addressed by the Working Party; this is surprising given the considerable significance of the defining activity of the police in this offence. The distinction between the 'fallen' woman and the 'respectable' woman does however require clarification if we are to understand not only the operation of the law but also the Working Party's report and its omissions. At the basis of the distinction between the prostitute and the respectable woman is the idea that the former is promiscuous in her sexuality, receiving payment for her services, while the latter is inclined towards monogamy and is not instrumental in her sexuality. Significantly there are no such contradictory categories that can be applied to men. A woman who is promiscuous in her sexuality is inevitably unrespectable while a man who behaves in a similar manner does not lose his respectability. In dealing with 'kerb crawlers' or men who attempt to make contact with prostitutes, the Working Party (like the Wolfenden Committee) notes that even though a man may be engaged in such an activity he may still be considered a 'respected member of the community'. Yet the very existence of the Working Party and its topic of investigation derives from the fact that if a woman behaves similarly she *cannot* remain a respected person; she automatically becomes a social outcast. In the (hetero)sexual sphere therefore we have two categories of women, the respectable and the 'fallen'; with men however the law appears to recognize only one category, the respectable. This is the fundamental basis of the discrimination against women embodied in the current Street Offences Act and while this anomaly remains it is impossible to maintain that the criminal law treats men and women equally.

Rape

The laws governing rape, both in the UK and the USA, are a

unique example of the way in which legal statute may discriminate against women, in this instance female victims of sexual assault, thereby making a nonsense of the claim of equal protection by the law for both sexes. The law on rape is discriminatory in at least two senses; first, in terms of its definition of the offence, namely as sexual intercourse with a woman by force, threat or fraud where the term 'woman' does not include wife,[1] and second, in terms of particular rules of evidence operative in rape cases. The rules of evidence create a situation in which rape becomes an offence for which the ratio of convictions to cases brought is much lower than generally holds for other offences. For example, taking the period from 1969 to 1974, the official criminal statistics for England and Wales reveal that on average the percentage of all proceedings against men for rape in Magistrates' and Crown Courts which end in convictions is 59·9 per cent. For the same period Crown Courts alone convicted 74·3 per cent of those on trial for rape while Magistrates' Courts, which deal with far fewer cases of rape, convicted 38·5 per cent of those heard by magistrates. Magistrates' Courts would appear to have a much lower rate of convictions for rape than Crown Courts; a record which cannot really be accounted for in terms of the seriousness of the offence as that would affect sentencing policy rather than conviction rates. In any case the number of convictions in all courts is not very high; if for example it is compared with the figures for assault by men over the period 1969 to 1974 we find that the average annual percentage of those proceeded against for assault which end in convictions is 96·8 per cent in Crown Courts and 85·3 per cent in Magistrates' Courts. Clearly a man accused of assault who is taken to court has a far greater chance of being convicted of the offence than a man charged with rape (see Appendices I and II).

We must remember that the number of rapes known to the police (see Table 5.1) and the number of men charged with rape are not equivalent to the total number of rapes occurring in any one year. For example for the period 1969 to 1974 the percentage of rapes known to the police resulting in court proceedings was 53·2 per cent. In other words little more than half of the rapes that are reported to the police result in a court appearance by a suspect. Of the same total of known rapes for the same period a mere 32 per cent resulted in convictions, so it can be seen that the chances of a conviction for rape are extremely small.

Table 5.1 *Rape offences recorded as known to the police and the number of Court proceedings started for rape offences*

Year	Number of offences of rape known to police	Number of males proceeded against for charges of rape
1969	869	468
1970	884	467
1971	784	437
1972	893	508
1973	998	501
1974	1,052	538

Source: *Home Office Official Statistics for England and Wales.*

Similar figures are available for the USA where Gilley (1974) estimates that only 56 per cent of reports of rape lead to arrest, only 62 per cent of arrests lead to a prosecution and only 36 per cent of prosecutions lead to a conviction. When it is considered that rape is a severely under-reported offence (Gilley estimates that only one in ten cases is known to the police in the USA) the conviction rate of 'actual' rapes is reduced to a figure of around 0·9 per cent. It is of course very difficult to speculate about the numbers of rapes which are not reported, especially in the UK where rape has not become such a significant issue in the Women's Movement as in the USA and where rape crisis centres are so few that only a minority of women might be encouraged to reveal that they have been raped. Nevertheless in the UK, as in the USA, it seems likely that the percentage of actual rapes which end in a conviction must be extremely small.

Superficially it may seem that the rules of evidence in rape cases have little to do with the reasons for rape being so under-reported or for explaining why the police bring so few suspected rapists to court. It might seem that these rules are operative only in court where they affect the conviction rates of those charged with rape.

However, this is not the case because the rules of evidence are so biased against the complainant that it is difficult to establish convictions for rape and this produces a situation in which the police tend to be reluctant to bring a case to trial where there is any uncertainty about the strength of the complainant's evidence. These unfair requirements of evidence also affect the decision to press charges by the potential prosecutrix[2] who may be unwilling to endure an embarrassing and humiliating cross-examination in public.

The element of the rules of evidence which is so significant in rape cases is the practical requirement of corroboration. There is no statutory legal requirement for corroborated evidence in rape trials in the UK although in practice it is extremely hard to secure a conviction without such evidence. Where the evidence is un-corroborated the judge must warn the jury that the evidence may be insufficient to convict and in practice juries are usually directed not to convict on the uncorroborated testimony of the complainant (cf. Cross, 1967). Exceptions may be made however; for example 'when the age of the victim renders it improbable that the charge was promoted by hysteria or spite, and an admission of indecency may dispense with the need for corroboration on a charge of indecent assault' (Cross, 1967, p. 174). Corroboration of evidence is therefore seen as a protection for the defendant against unjust accusations and this stems from the traditional belief that rape is a charge which is easy to make but difficult to defend. The genesis of this view is the belief that women are frequently vindic-tive enough to accuse falsely a man of rape in order to gain revenge or to protect herself in the light of premarital pregnancy. Yet in my discussion of rape in Chapter 4 I referred to the fact that rape is frequently a planned assault, involving more than one assail-ant; in the light of such evidence it is difficult to comprehend the belief that women falsely accuse their attackers. In addition existing evidence points to the reticence of the victim of a rape attack to report the offence and this conflicts with the assumption that women are inclined to falsely accuse out of spite (cf. Holm-strom and Burgess, 1975). Nevertheless such beliefs are incorpor-ated into legal practice and so corroboration of evidence is a vital issue in almost all rape trials in both the UK and the USA.

Corroboration of evidence requires that items of evidence which implicate the defendant are independent of the prosecutrix's testimony. In other words the complainant's testimony alone is rarely treated as sufficient evidence to convict a suspect, neither is evidence which supports her testimony—such as her telling her friends and neighbours she has been raped—considered sufficient. To corroborate evidence adequately a second witness to the rape or forensic and medical evidence are required. Corroboration may be required on three points, the identification of the assailant, penetration and consent. Which of these points becomes most significant in a rape trial depends on how the accused conducts his defence. If he applies a negative defence he denies all knowledge of the event and denies sexual intercourse. In this case corroboration is necessary for the points of identification and penetration. Separate medical evidence can often establish penetration, especially where it is forced or where the hymen is ruptured; it is not so easy however where the victim of a rape is prevented from resisting by threats of violence and who therefore may not be internally bruised or wounded. Identification is also possible through such means as fingerprints, shoe prints, hair and fibres, blood and other body fluids which may be matched to the accused (cf. Hibey, 1973). Each of these items of corroborative evidence can be supplied independently of the complainant's testimony. When the defendant applies a positive defence however he admits to the event and sexual intercourse so that matters of identification and penetration become insignificant. In such a case the defendant will maintain that the complainant consented to the intercourse and so the question of consent becomes of primary importance. It is of course much harder to establish separate corroborative evidence for the issue of consent and so most defence lawyers use this means of defending their clients. Rape, except for group or pair rapes, is unlikely to take place in public so witnesses to the event are rare. It is not sufficient that a woman should immediately inform others of the attack (i.e. rape crisis centres or doctors) because this is not treated as independent or corroborative evidence. The victim's testimony will be corroborated to some extent however if she is wounded and her clothes torn and dirty. Unfortunately, the victim's understandable first reaction after being raped is often to wash and change her clothing (if she is able to) before she informs others about the attack and this reduces the chances that her version of the event will be taken seriously. In fact the longer it takes for a rape to be reported the less likely it is that lack of consent will be believed and if the victim fails to make an official complaint consent will be assumed. Evidence of self-defence may help to corroborate a testimony but even where the assault is reported immediately such evidence may not be available. If a rapist threatens a woman with a weapon or even verbally she may not try to defend herself; ironically the police caution women against self-defence to avoid a rape becoming a murder case or to reduce the possibility of serious injury being inflicted. Yet without evidence of a struggle and bruising the victim has virtually no way of corroborating her evidence.

The rules of evidence place the victim of a rape in a disadvantageous position in yet another way. In rape cases it is allowed that evidence about the victim's past sexual or gynaecological experiences may have a bearing on the outcome of the trial. Hence the type of work a woman does; whether she is unmarried and on the pill; whether she has been sexually 'promiscuous'; whether she is in any way sexually liberated, may be treated as factors which have a bearing on the credibility of her testimony. One particular rape trial in the UK has had a significant bearing on the issue of the character of the complainant. In *R*. v. *Bashir and Manzir* the judge stated that,

Previous intercourse with the accused is, one would think, relevant to the question of consent although sexual intercourse with other men is not.... There is a difference between the woman who has acts of sexual intercourse with men and a prostitute who regularly sells her body. It has been held that evidence may be given that a woman complainant is of notoriously bad character for chastity (All England Law Reports, 1969, vol. 3, p. 692).

This ruling is not entirely clear because it does not indicate whether only prostitutes can be considered to be of 'notoriously bad character for chastity' or whether the defence is allowed to try to prove that any woman has a 'bad' sexual character. In practice it seems that defence lawyers do try to destroy the character of the complainant by reference to an 'unorthodox' sex life (cf. Coote and Gill, 1975). Of course what constitutes an orthodox or 'good' sex life is never at issue in such cases and there appears to be a tendency to believe that any woman who is considered 'unchaste' has asked to be sexually assaulted. The key factor in this issue is the belief that once a woman has agreed to sexual intercourse with a man (or several men) on previous occasions she is always open to his (or their) advances. The case of prostitutes and rape is the extreme example of this attitude. It is assumed that because a woman is a prostitute she has given up all rights to the self-determination of her body, hence it is almost impossible to prove rape against a prostitute. In fact the defendant is allowed to claim in court that he believes the prosecutrix to be a prostitute and to give his own reasons for this assumption. If his claim is accepted he is unlikely to be convicted of rape as the complainant's testimony will be assumed to be a falsehood. The outcome of a rape case can be seen therefore to depend more upon the character of the complainant than on the actual events of the rape and for this reason the prosecutrix may justifiably feel that she, rather than the accused, is on trial (cf. Griffin, 1971; Weis and Borges, 1973). In direct contrast evidence about the defendant's past sex life is not allowed in court; even if he has a record involving rape it would not be permissible to use such evidence because it is generally thought to influence the jury unfairly. This protection for the defendant is based on the principle that the outcome of a case should be decided upon by the 'facts' of the case and not extraneous evidence about the character or behaviour of the accused in other situations. This right is not allowed to the rape victim however because it is argued that her character has a bearing upon whether she is likely to have consented to the sexual intercourse. In all cases, except rape, the character of the accused may become a point of issue during a trial if the accused attempts to discredit the complainant or witnesses for the prosecution. In other words, in the case of a non-sexual assault by a man on a woman, if the accused argued in his defence that the woman was not a credible witness or that she had on previous occasions requested that he should assault her, the complainant would also be able to produce evidence that discredited the accused's character, such as a previous record of assaulting women. In rape cases the same principle of reciprocation is not allowed however. If the accused argues that the complainant is a 'loose' woman or that she has had intercourse with him before, the complainant may not reciprocate in kind with evidence of the accused's past sexual history or even his record of rape where applicable. Rape trials are unique therefore in that they do not offer the complainant the same rights as complainants in all other criminal proceedings.

The issue of criminal intent or *mens rea* is yet another reason for an even greater disadvantage to the complainant than the requirements of corroborated evidence. Even if a woman is able to prove that she did not consent to sexual intercourse this does not establish the guilt of the accused. It must be shown in court not only that the rape occurred but that it was the intention of the assailant to have intercourse in spite of, or with indifference to, the woman's desires. If the accused can show that he honestly believed the woman consented, even though this belief might be unreasonable, he cannot be guilty of rape because *mens rea* is absent. The element of *mens rea* is not peculiar to rape cases, for example with offences like shoplifting it is possible to defend oneself by denying the intention to steal. In addition the Criminal Justice Act 1967 established that a defendant cannot be convicted of any offence simply because his denial of criminal intent appears to be based on unreasonable foundations. This principle was firmly established in the case of rape in 1975, when the Law Lords ruled that the element of reason should not be significant in deciding the guilt of the accused. Prior to this decision there had been considerable confusion and ambiguity over whether the behaviour of the accused should be judged in terms of a hypothetical standard, such as an average reasonable man, or in terms of the accused's own powers of reason and comprehension. However, the principle has now been established that the accused must be shown to have honestly believed the complainant consented to sexual intercourse whether or not his belief is reasonable. In effect this has made rape a criminal act that need not have a perpetrator, for although a woman may have been raped the man who assaulted her is not guilty of rape if he can convince the jury of the honesty of his belief in her consent to sexual intercourse. The interests and rights of the woman and the man in such a case are clearly at odds and although it is against the principles of English law to convict a person who had no criminal intent when committing an offence this ruling by the Law Lords adds to the disadvantages faced by the victim of a rape in a court of law.

The Law Lords' ruling may, however, prove to be short lived. This is because the ruling created a great deal of public outrage which ultimately led the Home Secretary to set up the Advisory Group on the Law of Rape with specific instructions to consider the Law Lords' ruling and other matters relating to legal procedure and rape. The Advisory Group Report (1975) includes several recommendations for changes in the law, in particular where the rights of the prosecutrix are concerned. These recommendations include the drafting of a definition of rape to be set out in statutory form which would include a statutory provision to change the emphasis of the Law Lords' ruling such that the reasonableness of the accused's belief would be treated as directly pertaining to the honesty of his belief. They also include the right for the complainant to remain anonymous and suggest that there should be a balanced ratio of the sexes on juries dealing with rape cases. The remaining important recommendations in the report are more controversial. For example, although it is recommended that the previous sexual history of the complainant with other men should not be admissible, such evidence may be included at the judge's discretion. Consequently the judge might allow such evidence if he is satisfied

that this evidence relates to behaviour on the part of the complainant which was strikingly similar to her alleged behaviour on the occasion of, or in relation to, events immediately preceding or following the alleged offence (Report of the Advisory Group on the Law of Rape, 1975, p. 36).

This in effect means that the judge alone may decide what is relevant evidence and the so-called promiscuous woman or the prostitute may still find themselves at a considerable disadvantage should the judge maintain that their past sexual behaviour is indeed relevant. The Advisory Group appears to accept the principle that if a woman behaved in a certain way on one occasion it has a bearing on her behaviour in a separate situation.

The Report also includes a recommendation to allow evidence of the accused's bad character into court only under the circumstances which pertain in all criminal proceedings except where the judge has allowed for discreditory evidence against the complainant to be introduced. But the accused would still be able to refer to the complainant's sexual history, where it involves himself, with total impunity. The Advisory Group in fact accepts the principle that a previous sexual relationship between the accused and the complainant is significant to the issue of the woman's consent at the time in question. Again the assumption here appears to be that once a woman has consented to a sexual relationship with a man she is unlikely to dissent at a later stage. The prime example of this attitude is the law on rape pertaining to married couples which the Advisory Group overlooks entirely. Legally a man cannot rape his wife because she has given up the right to dissent to sexual intercourse on marriage. This legal deprivation of a woman's rights over her own body is summed up by Hale in the following statement:

the husband cannot be guilty of a rape committed by himself upon his lawful wife, for by their mutual matrimonial consent and contract the wife hath given up herself in this kind unto her husband which she *cannot retract* (Smith and Hogan, 1973, p. 324). (Emphasis added.)

The position of the wife who is raped by her husband or the girl who is raped by her boyfriend is therefore not significantly affected by the recommendations of the Advisory Group.

After the publication of the Advisory Group Report, a Private Member's Bill entitled the Sexual Offences (Amendment) Bill was introduced to Parliament. This Bill, which promises to become law in 1976, embodies many of the Advisory Group's recommendations on the law relating to rape. One important omission, however, is the requirement for an evenly balanced sex-ratio on juries in rape cases. The abandonment of this recommendation is a serious impediment to any attempt to improve the fairness of courtroom procedure for the victims of rape. In Chapter 4

I indicate that sexual mores, being different for men and women, influence attitudes towards rape such that where a conviction of rape depends mainly on the question of a woman's consent, men are more likely to be sympathetic with the accused than the complainant. A jury consisting mostly of men is therefore less likely to offer the complainant a comprehending 'audience', nor is it likely to instil her with confidence given that most courtroom officials, barristers and judges are also male. The victim of rape will therefore still feel extremely exposed and vulnerable in the courtroom environment.

In other respects the Bill broadly follows the Advisory Group Report and on becoming an Act of Parliament it will offer certain protections to the complainant in a rape case. It should be stressed however that the question of a woman's sexual history and relations with men other than the accused, and the recommendation for anonymity for the complainant, will depend upon the discretion of the Court. Where a judge feels that the repression of such information may be detrimental to the defendant's case he may allow such evidence or information to be used. Moreover, in the instance where a defendant is allowed to defame the character of the complainant, the complainant is still not allowed to reciprocate in kind by citing evidence of the defendant's sexual history or criminal record. Equally important is the fact that the Sexual Offences (Amendment) Bill allows the defendant to bring to court evidence of any past sexual relationship *he* may have had with the complainant. In common with the Advisory Group the Bill embraces the principle that women, once having had a sexual relationship with a particular man, are unlikely to dissent from further sexual encounters with him. Consequently, a woman who has had a sexual relationship with a man who later rapes her, cannot avoid the possibility that her sexual activities will be openly described in court. Significantly, though, a clause was added to the Bill which allows a wife to prosecute her husband if he should rape her, it being argued that a man should not have sexual rights over a woman merely because he is married to her. Unfortunately, this radical clause was short lived and the House of Commons swiftly rejected it because it threatened the legal and normative foundations of marriage and 'marital rights' in contemporary Western cultures.

Yet in spite of these major failings the Sexual Offences (Amendment) Bill will offer some improvement on the existing laws on rape when it becomes a legal statute. Most notably it modifies the Law Lords' ruling on *mens rea* and the question of whether reasonableness on the part of the accused's behaviour should be taken into account by the jury. Section 1(2) states,

It is hereby declared that if at a trial for a rape offence the jury has to consider whether a man believed that a woman was consenting to sexual intercourse, the presence or absence of reasonable grounds for such a belief is a matter to which the jury is to have regard, in conjunction with any other relevant matters, in considering whether he so believed (Sexual Offences (Amendment) Bill, 1975, p. 1).

In effect this reverses the emphasis of the Law Lords' ruling and therefore improves the situation for the rape victim. The extent to which other recommendations in the Bill, when they become law, will in fact ameliorate the post-rape experience of the complainant and will increase the conviction rates for rape is however still a matter for conjecture since it is well known that the principle or the spirit of a law is not always carried through in legal practice.

Women and the criminal process

Where the law can be seen to discriminate against women it is an inevitable consequence that the administration and enforcement of the law will reflect this lack of impartiality. For example in the case of rape the police are reluctant to prosecute the accused unless they have a corroborated testimony because they are aware of the difficulty of establishing a conviction without such evidence. But although the agents of law enforcement are obviously influenced in their actions by the laws they are obliged to maintain, a large area of discretion still exists in which individual or group attitudes become significant in the treatment of an offender or a victim. The police can exercise much discretion over which offences they choose to pursue and enforce and over how they deal with suspected offenders. Similarly probation officers and the courts are allowed a certain amount of discretion over the sentences they respectively recommend or impose. The conviction of rape, for example, carries with it a potential penalty of life imprison-

Table 5.2(a) *Typical sentences imposed for convictions of rape in Magistrates' Courts*

Sentence	1973	1974
Conditional discharge	—	6
Supervision order	1	3
Fine	4	2
Attendance Centre order	—	4
Detention Centre order	6	2
Care order	2	5
Commission for sentence under S.28 Magistrates' Court Act 1952	1	2
Total found guilty	14	24

Table 5.2(b) *Typical sentences imposed for convictions of rape in Crown Courts*

Sentence	1973	1974
Recognizance	1	—
Conditional discharge	—	5
Hospital order under S.60 Mental Health Act 1959	1	2
Restriction order under S.65 Mental Health Act 1959	9	6
Probation	9	8
Supervision order	1	1
Fine	4	1
Detention Centre	12	8
Borstal training	42	45
Suspended sentence	17	14
Imprisonment	216	224
Otherwise dealt with	2	3
Total found guilty	314	317

Table 5.2(c) *Typical length of prison sentence (immediate imprisonment)*
for convictions of rape in Crown Courts

Length of sentence	1973	1974
6 months and under	5	2
Over 6 months and up to 1 year	8	7
Over 1 year and up to 18 months	{ 27	10
Over 18 months and up to 2 years		18
Over 2 years and up to 3 years	64	75
Over 3 years and up to 4 years	44	49
Over 4 years and up to 5 years	32	28
Over 5 years and up to 7 years	25	17
Over 7 years and up to 10 years	8	8
Over 10 years	1	2
Life	2	8
Total found guilty	216	224

Source: *Official Criminal Statistics for England and Wales 1973 and 1974*,
Tables II and III.

ment but the courts rarely give the maximum possible sentence
and most usually give a penalty of two to three years' imprisonment[3] (see Table 5.2(a), (b) and (c)). It is within these areas of discretion that stereotyped perceptions of women, compounded by
popularized theories of female criminality and double-standards
of morality, can produce various forms of discrimination against
women.

The police officer, the probation officer and the judge are all
equally likely to be influenced by available common-sense explanations of female behaviour, and those among them who have been
exposed to theories of criminality during their training are likely
to have these conceptions confirmed by the traditional schools of
thought in criminology. The police officer who perceives the
prostitute to be a social outcast and a sexually deviant individual
who has limited civil rights *may* exploit such a situation and
attempt to degrade or humiliate, or simply unjustly arrest her (Dell,
1971; Winn, 1974). On the other hand the police officer who fails
to comprehend that women can be raped against their will or tends
to assume that false accusations are frequent occurrences, may be

less than understanding and sympathetic in his or her cross-examination of the victim. As Weis and Borges have pointed out, '[The rape victim] may experience the treatment by law enforcement agents as a degradation ceremony barely second to the actual rape' (op. cit., 1973, p. 103).

Such attitudes by agents of social control are most probably not universal but where they do occur they will be experienced as a form of discrimination which ultimately undermines the concept of 'impartial' justice. These unfavourable attitudes towards rape victims and prostitutes have their correlates in classical and contemporary theoretical accounts of female deviance. For example, Pollak (1961) warns against being deceived by false accusations of rape and he even refers to the accused rapist as the victim of the offence rather than the complainant. Similarly Davis (1971) argues that the individual prostitute is socially expendable, unlike her client, and being of low social status he considers it of little consequence for 'society' that she is frequently prosecuted. Davis and Pollak may be merely reflecting cultural attitudes towards women and sexual behaviour; nevertheless their work provides a scientific gloss for discriminatory practices against women. Such discrimination need not be overt or even intentional; indeed certain attitudes have become so taken-for-granted that they appear merely as a reflection of the natural order of things. Yet subtle and covert discrimination against particular members of society is no less a form of social injustice because it is not intended.

Pollak and several other criminologists (cf. Walker, 1973; Mannheim, 1965; Smith, 1974) have asserted that the enforcement and administration of the law treats women more favourably than men but a careful appraisal of the situation, especially in the area of so-called sexual offences, reveals certain anomalies and subtle forms of discrimination which have hitherto been overlooked. In Chapter 1 I discussed the way in which juvenile courts in the UK and the USA both over-emphasize the sexual behaviour of 'delinquent' girls and concentrate on the transgression of the moral code rather than the legal code. This concern with sexual morality is a reflection of our cultural attitudes towards the sexuality of young people, particularly females, and the preservation of the concept of a monogamous family structure in industrial societies and the concomitant belief in the need for sexual abstinence until marriage or a marriageable age. The requirement for celibacy however has traditionally been a reality only for women and girls who have had to bear the consequences of premarital sexual intercourse, whilst in contrast men and boys have been encouraged to gain sexual experience before marriage. Although sexual mores are changing, allowing for a greater freedom of sexual experience for women, the legal and judicial systems have been slow in responding to such developments and tend to be reformed only in the wake of public opinion. Consequently a dual-standard of morality still operates in legal and judicial processes, sexual (mis)behaviour in women and girls being more heavily sanctioned than the same (mis)behaviour in men and boys. Girls committing sexual misdemeanours (they are not classed as offences in the UK) are therefore far more likely to be placed in institutions than either girls committing non-sexual offences or boys committing sexual misdemeanours or non-sexual offences. For example, in her study of female delinquency in the Bristol and Bath areas between 1969 and 1972 Smith (1975) found that the nature of the offences committed by adolescent girls was directly related to the severity of subsequent punishment or treatment. She maintains

Girls in need of Care and Protection and control and known to have indulged in sexual intercourse under age were seven times more likely to be incarcerated than those convicted of what may be termed 'criminal offences'. The relationship was still significant when class background was held constant (Smith, 1974, p. 5).

Similarly in the USA, Terry (1970) found that the juvenile courts treat girls who have been involved in (potentially) sexual exploits more severely than girls committing other types of offences. His study also indicates that sexually 'delinquent' girls are more heavily sanctioned than boys regardless of the nature of the boys' offences or the length of their previous criminal record.

The influence of the traditional double-standard of morality may not be restricted to the sentencing policy of the juvenile courts, indeed there is evidence to suggest that probation officers may be similarly influenced. In a study of probation officers in the

Bronx (New York) Children's Court, Cohn (1970) found that although girls formed a minority of offenders in the study, they were three times as likely to be recommended for institutionalization by probation officers than the boys. Moreover most of these girls had committed acts which were described as sexually delinquent and Cohn argues that this was a decisive factor in the probation officers' recommendations of institutionalization. The type of offence committed by the adolescent girls in Cohn's study was also an important factor where decisions involved the recommendation of a psychiatric examination. She states, 'The fact that girls committed acts against sexual taboos or against parents was enough, apparently, to lead the probation officer to assume that psychiatric help was needed' (Cohn, 1970, p. 202). This attitude towards female delinquency reflects the commonly held belief that deviancy by a female is a sign of a much deeper pathology than deviancy by a male. It also illustrates the fact that there is a tendency to treat the incidence of sexual delinquency in girls as more serious than other forms of delinquent behaviour. Cohn's study is not a definitive work however, and there are several dangers involved in attempting to generalize from her work about the attitudes of probation officers. In particular it seems that the existence of a broken home, in addition to the nature of the offence committed by a girl, constitutes an important factor in the decision-making process of probation officers. This position is also implied by Smith (1975), namely that broken homes are a significant factor in the sentencing policy by the juvenile courts in the UK. Where there is a broken home it seems that the authorities feel it is necessary to place a girl into institutional care because of the protection it affords. This reasoning is however itself a consequence of differential perceptions of the sexual behaviour of boys and girls, perceptions producing a situation in which girls are treated as though they are in need of protection either from their own or others' sexuality. This kind of reference to protection also implies a paternalism in the authorities' attitude towards 'delinquent' girls, but paternalism may merely serve to disguise a more severe degree of punishment thought to be appropriate for adolescent promiscuity. For example, Cowie, Cowie and Slater, in their study of a classifying school, maintain 'These girls had to be removed from society into the security of a residential school much more for their own sakes than to protect society' (Cowie *et al.*, 1968, p. 166). What is neglected in such an explanation is that girls and boys who have committed 'criminal' offences are sent to the same or similar institutions creating a situation in which sexual delinquency appears, in terms of punishment, to be equated with criminal behaviour. Moreover, the idea of institutionalizing individuals for their protection or because of their potential delinquency is itself controversial. It is not a circumstance that is permissible in the treatment of adult offenders and it represents a contradiction of the principles of English law, namely the assumption of innocence and the judicial establishment of guilt for an offence which has been committed. However, juvenile courts have in some respects much wider powers than criminal courts and as they are not restricted to the area of the criminal law they may also deal with moral infractions where no legal offence is committed. Unfortunately it is within this 'grey' area of morality that female 'delinquents' are most at risk, and where the differential evaluation of girls' and boys' sexual behaviour has the most profound consequences.

Adolescent girls in the UK are most frequently placed in institutions because they are classified as being in need of Care and Protection. Circumstances which may be regarded as warranting Care and Protection include being exposed to moral danger, being beyond parental control, truanting or being ill-treated. This represents a picture very similar to that found in the USA where Vedder and Sommerville (1970) have listed the predominant juvenile 'offences' by girls leading to commitment as running away, incorrigibility, sexual offences, probation violation and truancy. With the exception of 'being in moral danger' (in the UK) and sexual offences (in the USA) these 'offences' do not appear to be of a sexual nature. Yet frequently the underlying assumption in these cases is one of sexual misconduct resulting in severe disapprobation for female offenders. For example the Ingleby Committee on Children and Young Persons (1960) provides evidence of the strong disapproval of many agents of social control when confronted by girls who are classified as being in need of Care and Protection. In their evidence to the Ingleby Committee the

Association of Headmasters, Headmistresses and Matrons of Approved Schools state:

A more serious problem is presented by girls, often committed at a very late date as 'in need of Care and Protection'. In our view this term is wrongly used as they are not usually innocent victims of circumstances, but girls of shallow personality to whom promiscuous living appears attractive. They are often completely anti-social, absconding, refusing training and committing further offences (Richardson, 1969, p. 84).

Technically however, children who are institutionalized for truancy, being in moral danger or being beyond parental control, are non-offenders as they have had no criminal offence proved against them. This produces a situation in which our Approved Schools (now Community Homes) contain both officially designated offenders and non-offenders. In 1960 the Ingleby Committee established the proportions of non-offenders and offenders present in juvenile establishments and found that for boys, 95 per cent who were institutionalized were classed as offenders and only 5 per cent were non-offenders. The analysis of girls in such institutions revealed a very different situation however, because only 36 per cent were offenders while a majority of 64 per cent were non-offenders. It seems therefore that far more juvenile female non-offenders are placed in institutions than male non-offenders and this may well reflect the different degrees of seriousness attributed to the same or similar non-criminal behaviour in boys and girls. The Ingleby Committee has attempted to justify this apparently discriminatory policy by referring to the criminal potential of many promiscuous girls. They state:

Almost all adolescent girls sent to approved schools (whether as offenders or not) have a history of sexual immorality, and many of those sent as being in need of care or protection or beyond control are known to have committed offences (Richardson, 1969, p. 84).

The point that is overlooked by the Committee, however, is that if these girls had been brought to court for criminal offences rather than for behaviour related to sexual promiscuity, they would have been far more likely to have received a non-custodial sentence and therefore a less severe punishment. Moreover the Committee presumes guilt on the behalf of these adolescent girls where guilt has not been proven. It would be hard to justify the incarceration of adults on the grounds that they are 'known' to have committed offences if their guilt had not been legally established in a court of law. The belief that girls who are institutionalized for being in need of Care and Protection are also criminal offenders, and the assumption that this justifies their overrepresentation in institutions, is quite unwarranted and represents an important illustration of the authorities' attitudes towards so-called 'wayward' girls.

Since the Ingleby Committee met in 1960 the Children and Young Persons Act of 1969 has formally abolished the distinction between offenders and non-offenders in the ten to seventeen year old age group as far as 'treatment' is concerned. Nevertheless in juvenile courts a distinction is still made in terms of the reasons for a court appearance so it is still quite possible for a girl being brought before the magistrates for being exposed to moral danger to compare her situation with a girl who has committed an offence. In this case she may justifiably feel she is being 'punished' for sexual 'promiscuity'.

Clearly more studies of the criminal process and the treatment of female offenders and non-offenders are necessary before we can reach firm conclusions concerning the basis of the differential treatment of boys and girls. The existing evidence from studies in both the UK and the USA does however indicate that where sexual offences are concerned female offenders are at a disadvantage; women being most at risk when they are prostitutes and girls when they are 'promiscuous'. This evidence contradicts the general claim that female offenders are more leniently treated than their male counterparts, although a qualification is in order here, namely that this refutation holds only in the case of sexual (mis)behaviour. Where offences against the person or against property are concerned there does not appear to be the same kind or degree of discrimination against women. In fact evidence *seems* to indicate that where property offences are involved, women are more leniently treated than men and similarly that girls are more readily cautioned, rather than prosecuted, by the police than boys. For example Walker (1973) has assessed the variation in sentencing of shoplifters, basing his figures on Gibbens and Prince's (1962) study of shoplifters in London in 1959. He found that 21 per cent of 234 male shoplifters were sentenced to imprisonment while only 4 per cent of 532 female shoplifters were similarly sentenced. However, these statistics may be misleading as they give no indication of the relative seriousness of the thefts by the men and women concerned. Moreover, as Walker points out, 49 per cent of the men had a record of previous convictions while this was true of only 20 per cent of the women. As the courts take into account the existence of a criminal record when considering the length of sentence, this factor is of considerable importance. The length of a criminal record is also important as one previous offence is unlikely to be treated as seriously as two or more offences and yet Walker does not indicate the relative length of previous records when he compares men and women with past convictions. Further studies able to account for such variables as previous convictions, the seriousness of the offence and home and personal circumstances must be conducted before definitive statements can be made about the relative leniency of the courts towards women convicted of property offences or violence against the person. The evidence which exists at present is inadequate to sustain the assertion that men are treated more severely than women by the courts.

The question of whether or not different policies exist for the cautioning of male and female offenders is also as yet unanswered, the available evidence provided by Walker to show that female offenders are more likely to be cautioned than their male counterparts is not satisfactory. (See Table 5.3 for the statistical evidence presented by Walker allegedly revealing the more favourable treatment of female offenders by the police.) Walker presents the number of offenders cautioned as a percentage of all those cautioned or found guilty of an offence in 1961; consequently it appears that proportionately more women are cautioned. Yet because far fewer women than men are convicted of offences this proportionate representation is biased against women. The use of this method of calculation creates a situation in which, even

Table 5.3   *Offenders cautioned as a percentage of those cautioned or found guilty in 1961*

Age group	Indictable offences		Non-indictable, non-motoring offences	
	Males	*Females*	*Males*	*Females*
8–13 years	28	40	36	47
14–16 years	14	22	25	27
17–20 years	6	8	7	36
21 and over	3	8	7	24

Source: Walker (1973), *Crime and Punishment in Britain*.

if the actual numbers of men and women cautioned were equal, their respective percentage figures would necessarily vary greatly. Because far greater numbers of men than women are convicted of offences the proportion of numbers cautioned against those convicted and cautioned is bound to be smaller than the proportion of women. A more reliable method of assessing policies for cautioning offenders is to take the numbers cautioned as a percentage of the total population. This is the method employed in the Official Statistics for England and Wales in making a comparison of males and females officially cautioned and found guilty of criminal offences. Table 5.4 shows the number of cautions by sex and age as a proportion of the total male and female population in each age group. This table indicates the converse of Walker's proposition; it reveals that far fewer females as a proportion of the total population, as compared to males, are cautioned. We must however be cautious about drawing conclusions from either Walker's or the Home Office statistics because, once again, we have no knowledge of the relative seriousness of the offences concerned, in what circumstances the offences were defined as offences by the police, or the criteria employed by the police in their decision to caution rather than prosecute.

The overriding problem with much of the existing work on the discretion of the police and courts in their treatment of offenders is that it presumes the existence of an attitude of benevolence and chivalry on the part of law enforcement agencies towards female

Table 5.4 *Persons cautioned for indictable offences per 100,000 of the population, by sex and age*

Age and Year	Persons cautioned per 100,000 of the population in the age group	
	Male	*Female*
Under 14:		
1971	1,962	479
1972	2,105	603
1973	2,166	646
1974	2,408	771
14 and under 17:		
1971	2,060	586
1972	2,198	679
1973	2,341	704
1974	2,773	863
17 and under 21:		
1971	283	41
1972	273	46
1973	284	45
1974	256	49
21 and under 30:		
1971	65	22
1972	67	23
1973	65	24
1974	60	22
30 and over:		
1971	23	20
1972	25	23
1973	25	21
1974	26	23
Totals:		
1971	308	80
1972	333	97
1973	347	100
1974	396	119

Source: *Official Criminal Statistics for England and Wales, 1974*, Table 5.

offenders. Previous studies have failed to distinguish between the types or categories of offences and have relied too heavily on incomplete and unreliable statistical sources with the result that the initial presuppositions receive confirmation and the complexity of the situation remains unrecognized. A critical approach to the often stated and implied belief in the favourable treatment of women by the agents of law enforcement is therefore scientifically necessary; certainly until further studies are completed such beliefs[4] should be viewed with scepticism.

Women and the penal system

There are several studies of women in prison (cf. Giallombardo, 1966; Ward and Kassebaum, 1966; Heffernan, 1972; Smith, 1962) and also studies of girls in institutions (cf. Richardson, 1969; Giallombardo, 1974; Konopka, 1966) which have analysed the social relationships between institutionalized offenders and have described the pains of imprisonment experienced by women and girls when committed to penal institutions. In many of these studies it is argued that imprisonment is an inappropriate form of punishment for female offenders; it is maintained that women suffer more hardships than men while they are in prison, largely because of their greater need for family life and the deleterious consequences of enforced separation from their children. In this section I shall not however be addressing arguments for and against the imprisonment of women or attempting to evaluate the hardships of institutional life; rather I shall focus on the role such institutions play in not only confirming the traditional dependent position of women in society but also in perpetuating the images of female offenders comparable to those found in classical and contemporary studies of female criminality.

Most regimes employed in penal institutions for female offenders are typically those which reinforce the stereotypical, traditional sex role of women in our culture. Inmates are usually given the opportunity to learn to sew, cook and do other domestic tasks, and in more liberal regimes they may be able to learn to type or take educational courses. As the average length of stay in an institution for a female offender is so short, vocational training is often not considered to be worth while and so inmates are rarely given the opportunity to gain qualifications that might help them to find employment (other than manual work) on release. Where facilities for 'useful' training do exist only a minority are usually able to benefit; this is a consequence of the scarcity of the necessary resources. But neither short sentences nor scarce resources fully account for the lack of vocational training in such penal institutions, rather it is a direct consequence of the attitude of policy-makers responsible for the allocation of resources that prevents female offenders from getting the opportunity to gain skills that might improve their opportunities on leaving prison. Hall-Williams (1970) describes this negative attitude towards the potential of female offenders:

[I]t is not seen as necessary or desirable to give women prisoners training for semi-skilled jobs. ... In any case, the quality of the population is not thought to call for any tasks other than fairly simple repetitive tasks, such as assembling kits of stationery requisites, placing coloured pencils, rubber and ruler into a plastic case, putting labels on a cardboard carton (Hall-Williams, 1970, p. 244).

It would seem from this statement that policy-makers believe that women in prison are not worth, or capable of, retraining. Women have little opportunity therefore of learning how to escape from their doubly socially inferior position while in prison.[5] On the contrary their dependent position in society is confirmed with the result that on release their ability to be self-determining and independent will not be improved. The only legitimate opportunities open to women with both a criminal record and training in 'assembling kits of stationery requisites' will be the lowest paid manual or domestic jobs or a return to the dependent status of housewife.

One reason why female offenders are not offered greater opportunities in prison is probably that women and girls are not perceived to be potential 'breadwinners' or in need of meaningful and remunerative employment.[6] Certainly similar arguments are proposed in other institutions where training facilities for women and girls are lacking or where boring low-paid work is predominantly carried out by female employees. However, there may also be a latent rationale for re-confirming the traditional role and status of women within penal institutions. This rationale is based on the assumption that the woman who accepts her traditional role, who is passive, gentle and caring, is also non-criminal. Conversely the rationale assumes that the emancipated woman is masculine in her attitudes and behaviour and consequently more likely to act in a criminal fashion. Seen in this light the policy of re-confirming the traditional role of women, the training in domestic or basic manual skills only, is an attempt to prevent recidivism and to rehabilitate the female offender into a socially approved non-criminal role.

Girls in juvenile institutions are likely also to experience similar attitudes towards their abilities and potentials as those expressed by Hall-Williams in respect of adult offenders. A typical example of this is the Approved School studied by Richardson (1969) where the girls had to do a variety of tasks from sewing to cleaning. She states,

Nine or ten girls were allocated each day to the household tasks, and as far as possible orderly succession was adhered to, so that a girl learned jobs of graded difficulty (from corridor scrubbing to dormitory cleaning; to turning out staff bedrooms, and finally serving meals or tea and coffee to staff) (Richardson, 1969, p. 25).

The educational provision at the Approved School was very poor; the morning school was attended only by fourteen-year-olds, newcomers and those who were 'inept' at practical tasks, while the afternoon school, which was attended by most girls, consisted of one hour of outdoor games and one hour of needlework. Consequently the Approved School tended to lend confirmation to stereotypical 'feminine' roles for girls in its care, giving them little opportunity for self-fulfilment in less 'conventional' areas. In fact any 'masculine' aspirations were frowned upon and more appropriate 'feminine' occupations were encouraged. For example Richardson maintains that 'One girl whose expressed interests at the Classifying School had been boyish in the extreme, with ambitions to be a footballer, naturally looked rounder and softer six months later when she wanted to be a hairdresser' (Richardson, 1969, p. 58). Such attitudes towards gender-appropriate roles are not peculiar to the Approved School studied by Richardson, rather they are typical of the attitudes to be found not only in similar institutions but in society in general, although it should be noted that some measure of progress, albeit small, is occurring in ordinary schools (cf. DES Education Survey 21, 1975).

At the same time as encouraging 'feminine' role behaviour like cooking and sewing for girls in juvenile institutions there is also a tendency to be critical of 'feminine' emotional reactions, such as being hysterical, or 'feminine' interests such as hair-styling, fashionable clothes or cosmetics. Hence girls are expected to be 'feminine' in respect of their domestic role but not 'feminine' in respect of their sexual role. This creates a double-bind situation for many institutionalized girls because while they are given no option but to act in a stereotypically 'feminine' way, when they adopt this role to the full they are seen as 'unbalanced', 'promiscuous' or 'silly'. In an important respect such girls experience all the disadvantages of the traditional female role (i.e. drudgery, boredom, limited horizons) without the 'advantages' (i.e. romance, flirtation and sexual encounters). Richardson has unwittingly given an example of the double-bind situation faced by many girls in institutions by drawing attention to the fact that 'feminine' behaviour is encouraged (although 'masculine' behaviour is *respected*) but that the expression of sexuality is constrained. In describing a particular incident she states:

A stalwart who worked hard in the garden one winter's day and left on the gardener's bicycle, typified more the delinquent boy, and the change was relished. When she later played the prostitute in a US camp, she had reduced her stature in staff eyes (op. cit., 1969, p. 43).

Similarly, Richardson implies a criticism of the girls for their 'dopey appearance', lack of grace and refinement while on the other hand being critical of them for the time spent in front of a mirror because it disrupts the rigid timetable of the school. This double-bind situation means ultimately that girls are punished for not being 'feminine' enough as well as for being too 'feminine'.

Penal institutions for female offenders do not only support the traditional and inferior social position of women and girls, they reflect in good part the assumptions inherent in the work of several criminologists (i.e. Lombroso and Ferrero, 1895; Glueck and Glueck, 1934; Cowie *et al.*, 1968), namely that women and girls who commit offences are abnormal either biologically or psychologically. The confirmation or 'proof' of this abnormality is usually said to be inherent in the fact that these women and girls commit offences; their deviancy is treated as a manifestation of the existence of some form of mental or physiological imbalance. This basic assumption of the abnormality of the female offender appears to be the major premise of recent changes in penal policy. In particular the transformation of Holloway Prison into a psychiatric hospital seems indicative of a new approach to the problem of female criminality which is dependent upon the adoption of a belief that the offender is, in some way, 'sick'. The new Holloway will be staffed with doctors and nurses as well as prison officers who will be encouraged to adopt a welfare role (cf. Faulkner, 1971). The inmates will experience treatment based on group therapy, group counselling and group living, although where resources and time are scarce supplementary programmes of drug and electro-convulsive treatment may be implemented (cf. Radical Alternatives to Prison, 1974). The new Holloway will provide no vocational training or remunerative work; instead 'therapeutic' and domestic work will be provided, in this respect the new Holloway will differ little from other established penal institutions for women.

The aim of the programme of treatment in Holloway will be to achieve conformity in its inmates through modifying their personalities and attitudes. In embracing such a goal the role of the legal system, the police and courts, as well as an inequitable social system, in the process of criminalization, is entirely ignored. Moreover, the treatment programme may also be indicative of a change in the conception of the motivational basis of criminality away from the classical concept of responsibility towards a more positivistic orientation which emphasizes individual pathology. In this respect changes in penal policy appear to reflect trends in criminological theories about female criminality which also adhere to a pathological model. Apparently policy-makers, like many criminologists, perceive female criminality as irrational, irresponsible and largely unintentional behaviour, as an individual maladjustment to a well-ordered and consensual society. Yet as well as sharing basic assumptions, criminological theories of female criminality may serve to legitimize the trends in penal policy, giving scientific justifications for the treatment of female offenders as 'sick' individuals. Such legitimization follows from the confirmation of certain cultural understandings of female behaviour in general and criminal behaviour in particular and is a consequence of the failure of criminological theorists to explicate or treat as topics for analysis the understandings which they share with those engaged in the formulation of social policy.

Chapter 6

Women, crime and mental illness

In discussing the phenomena of female criminality and mental illness[1] in women I shall concentrate on two major propositions which regularly occur in the literature dealing with these issues. The first proposition raises the question of the motivational basis of female offenders' actions, the inference being that female offenders are mentally ill or 'sick' in a psychological sense. The second proposition revolves around the idea that mental illness for women represents an equivalent or alternative form of behaviour to criminality. The latter proposition presupposes that because statistically speaking more women are diagnosed as mentally ill than become categorized as criminal, mental illness is a form of deviant behaviour appropriate to women, fulfilling for them the same needs or functions as criminal behaviour does for men. These two controversial propositions will be discussed in turn.

The sickness model of female criminality

There is a tendency in the English penal system towards associating criminal behaviour with mental instability and non-rational motivation, a development which is not peculiar to the analysis of female criminality. For example, there is a psychiatric prison, Grendon Underwood, for male offenders (although this particular institution deals with only a minority of imprisoned offenders), and there are psychiatric wings in many ordinary prisons (e.g. Wormwood Scrubs). However, the assumption of relationship between criminality and 'sickness' of a psychological nature appears to be most relevant in the case of conventional understandings of, and treatment recommended for, female offenders. The identification of mental instability or irrationality as an important factor in the generation of female criminality is more a consequence of the relative infrequency of criminal activity by women than a result of a genuine understanding of the etiology of female crime. As Walker states,

Certainly in practice women offenders have a higher chance of being dealt with as mentally abnormal. . . . We cannot however exclude the possibility that psychiatrists' diagnoses . . . are being influenced by the . . . proposition . . . that there is probably something abnormal about a woman delinquent (Walker, 1973, p. 302).

The basic assumption inherent in this proposition is that the unusual is necessarily abnormal or unnatural and consequently female offenders, who have always been insignificant in statistical terms, are perceived as 'sick'. The redevelopment of Holloway from a prison to a psychiatric hospital is itself a concrete manifestation of this type of understanding of female criminality. Moreover the fact that Holloway receives about half of the total number of female prisoners in England and Wales means that, even though it is only one institution, it is comparatively more significant than the remaining penal institutions for women. The change in Holloway establishes a major shift in penal policy concerning women. Indeed, on completion of the rebuilding of Holloway, about half of the female offenders who are sentenced to imprisonment will be placed in an institution whose stated policy is psychiatric in orientation, emphasizing the treatment of inmates and concentrating on their individual needs and psychological problems.

Inherent in this pathological model of female criminality are important implications for both our understanding of the nature of criminality and the treatment of offenders. First, this model presumes criminal action to be irrational, illogical and without meaning for the actor. Second, the socio-economic structure of society is seen to have little or no influence on the nature or degree of criminal activity, except where it can be said to have a 'triggering' effect on the pathological mind. Crime is therefore seen as an individual rather than a social phenomenon with the consequence that attention is devoted to 'treatment' focused on the individual rather than directed towards changing underlying social conditions. Third, it denies the significance of the will or intention of the actor, and lastly it fails to address to socio-cultural and historical basis of the legal definition of crime.

The consequences of adopting the 'sick' analogy may affect both male and female offenders, but it is arguably more serious for women in a society where common-sense understandings of personality differences between men and women lead to the latter being perceived as less rational, less intelligent and less self-directing than men. In other words, women 'fit' more easily into the model provided by the 'sick' analogy because of the cultural stereotype pertaining to women. Moreover in terms of subsequent treatment women may also be in a more vulnerable position than men. Chesler (1974) points out that many studies have been conducted to discover the effects on an individual of being treated as an irrational, immature, 'sick' being in various kinds of institutions, but the effects of such treatment on women in particular have not been seriously considered. She states,

Like most people, [Goffman] is primarily thinking of the debilitating effect—*on men*—of being treated like a woman (as helpless, dependent, sexless, unreasonable—as 'crazy'). But what about the effects of being treated like a woman when you *are* a woman? And perhaps a woman who is already ambivalent or angry about just such treatment? (Chesler, 1974, p. 35).

Such treatment can therefore be seen to represent a double burden for women. Moreover, with the growing influence of psychological ideas on penal policy, the existence of a double-standard of mental health for men and women within established psychology provides legitimate cause for concern. This double standard has recently been studied by Dr I. K. Broverman *et al.* (1970) who prepared a questionnaire in which seventy-nine clinicians (psychiatrists, psychologists and social workers; forty-six male and thirty-three female) had to rate certain bipolar traits as representing healthy male, healthy female or healthy adult (sex unspecified) behaviour. The results showed that for all the clinicians, irrespective of sex, the concept of a healthy male approximated closely to that of the healthy adult. However, their concept of healthy, mature women differed significantly from those for men and adults; in general women were described as more excitable in minor crises, more easily hurt, more emotional, more submissive, less independent, and so on. Moreover a separate study carried out with non-professional subjects indicated that personality traits that were judged as 'socially desirable' correlated very closely with the traits selected by the clinicians as healthy male and healthy adult traits. However, the socially undesirable traits resembled those judged by the clinicians to be characteristic of the female personality. We can observe therefore that the normal healthy woman, as perceived by these clinicians, is not a healthy adult and furthermore, according to common-sense criteria, she does not have socially desirable characteristics. Thus it seems that to be a healthy woman the individual must be a 'sick' adult and to be a healthy adult she must be a 'sick' woman—no wonder that women fit so easily into the sick analogy!

The consequences of providing treatment programmes for women based on such clinical judgments and assumptions are serious. This is particularly the case when the treatment of women who are diagnosed as mentally ill or unbalanced is oriented towards their resocialization into their 'correct' social role, because this social role, as perceived by psychologists and others, is not a universally acceptable or an inherently natural role for women. It is, on the contrary, a culturally imposed role which becomes increasingly inadequate and stressful as more women question their position in society. Resocializing women into a stereotyped feminine role which is no longer acceptable to many women is no solution to the stress that such a role itself manifests. It is after all quite conceivable that it is the untenable nature of the traditional feminine role in the first place that produces a high incidence of breakdown among women.

Mental illness as a functional equivalent to criminal behaviour

Mental illness or imbalance may not only be treated as con-comitant with criminal behaviour in women, it is also frequently conceived as a functional alternative to crime. This thesis is based on the premise that deviant behaviour in men takes the form of criminal behaviour whilst in women it takes the form of mental breakdown. As Bertrand argues, 'Mental illness as an alternative or female equivalent to male antisocial and aggressive behaviour could be explored as a promising (partial) explanation of the female crime rate and of the nature of female criminality' (Bertrand, 1973, p. 17). However, before this possible explanation of female criminality and mental illness can be pursued there are some fundamental assumptions in the thesis which require clarification. The first is the assumption that women do in fact suffer more from mental illness than men. If it can be shown that women are no more likely to experience mental illness than men there is no basis to the supposition that mental illness is a 'female' form of deviance. The second assumption (where more women than men are diagnosed as suffering from mental illness) involves the elevation of psychiatric diagnosis to the level of an objective assessment of the mental health of women. In other words, it is assumed that the official rates of mental breakdown in the general population are a 'true' reflection of the mental health of the population, rather than the result of differential diagnosis based upon such factors as socio-economic class, sex or ethnicity. These two assumptions require closer examination before the thesis of the functional equivalence of criminality and mental illness can be adequately considered.

Mental illness in men and women

The problem of assessing whether more women have mental break-downs or suffer more from mental illness than men is how to define and recognize this breakdown or illness. Clearly any reliance on official statistics is going to be subject to the same criticisms that have been made of official criminal statistics. In particular such statistics cannot be assumed to give an accurate impression of what occurs in the 'real' world because the individual judgment and bureaucratic structures through which they are mediated in the process of codification and categorization distort the 'facts' in question. It is also the case that, just as official criminal statistics cannot account for the incidence of hidden crime or differential arrest and sentencing, official mental health statistics cannot account for undiscovered or undiagnosed mental breakdown and differential diagnosis and commitment to hospital. It is therefore inadvisable to depend uncritically on these statistics for any general statements about the differential rates of breakdown for men and women. However, the statistics are useful for showing the numbers of women and men actually admitted to psychiatric hospitals, how they are diagnosed, by whom they are referred, and so on. Estimates of the greater or lesser likelihood of women breaking down that are based on these statistics are highly tenuous though, in the same way that hypotheses on criminal behaviour based on prison populations are considered to be limited. In this section I will analyse the statistical information on mental illness and will consider in particular those studies that accept such statistical information as an unproblematic premise for explaining the perceived high rate of mental breakdown of women.

The Department of Health and Social Security Inpatient Statistics for Psychiatric Hospitals and Units in England and Wales for the years 1968–71 do show a higher rate of commitment for women than men, as based on categories of mental health defined in the Mental Health Act 1959 (see Table 6.1). The sudden decline in first admissions shown in the figures for 1970 and 1971 can be

Table 6.1   *Mental illness hospitals and units under Regional Hospital Boards and Teaching Hospitals. Admissions by sex (England and Wales)*

Year	No. of admissions (all ages)				Admission rates per 100,000 home population			
	First*		Non first†		First		Non first	
	Male	Female	Male	Female	Male	Female	Male	Female
1968	38,124	55,754	34,403	50,740	161	223	146	203
1969	39,060	56,159	35,480	51,561	164	224	149	206
1970	28,053	39,671	46,848	68,782	118	158	197	273
1971	27,272	38,623	47,914	69,664	115	154	202	278

* First refers to first admission.
† Non first refers to non-first admission.

accounted for by a different method of assessment which was introduced in 1970. It is believed by the DHSS that the figures for 1970 and 1971 are therefore more 'accurate'. The figures listed under non-first admissions are also somewhat misleading because they include transfers between hospitals such that each time a patient is moved he, or she, will be counted again. Of course there is no way of telling from the statistics whether there is any variation between sexes or between diagnostic categories in the transference of patients.

From the available statistics it can be seen that there are more female in-patients in psychiatric hospitals and units than there are male. Furthermore statistics classifying by age as well as by sex show that after the age of ten years males at no time exceed the numbers of female inmates. The figures in Table 6.2, which are also based on DHSS in-patient statistics for psychiatric hospitals

Table 6.2   *Mental illness hospitals and units under Regional Hospital Boards and Teaching Hospitals*
   Admissions by sex and age: numbers and rates per 100,000 home population (England and Wales)

Age group	Admissions		Rates per 100,000 population	
	Male	*Female*	*Male*	*Female*
All ages	75,186	108,287	317	432
0–	673	270	16	7
10–	755	649	40	36
15–	3,566	4,598	208	280
20–	7,737	8,776	413	474
25–	14,467	18,469	465	610
35–	13,340	17,510	464	616
45–	13,137	18,114	444	593
55–	9,771	15,348	356	506
65–	6,991	13,091	403	542
75 and over	4,749	11,462	666	747

Source: *DHSS Inpatient Statistics for Psychiatric Hospitals and Units in England and Wales.*

and units in England and Wales, are typical. These statistics show what is virtually a reversal of the pattern of involvement by sex shown in the official criminal statistics. In other words men are more highly involved in crime than women but women are much more subject to mental illness than men. It must be restated however that statistics are not a 'true' reflection of the numbers of people actually involved in such activities even if they do represent the official picture.

In both the UK and the USA there have been attempts to explain this phenomenon but before discussing these studies it should be noted that there is a long tradition within psychology in general, and psychoanalysis in particular, which has taken women as the main focus of clinical research. Long before the existence of regular and thoroughly collated statistical 'evidence' women have been diagnosed as being more biologically or psychically oriented towards mental instability than men. In particular the Freudian school has concentrated on female patients, arguing that the fundamental cause of neurosis among women is their inability to come to terms with their biology and their un-avoidable feminine destiny (cf. Mitchell, 1974; J. Baker Miller, 1974). Yet it is perhaps even more significant that psychiatrists of the reputedly radical anti-psychiatry school, notably Laing and Esterson (1970), also concentrate on women and girls as the most suitable subjects for analysis (cf. Chesler, 1974). The question is whether this concentration is justified and, allowing that it is for the present, whether an adequate explanation is available to account for women's greater vulnerability to mental illness.

As it has provided an explanation of female criminality so biological and psychological determinism has also been used to explain women's perceived greater propensity towards mental instability. In Freudian analysis 'penis envy' in women is inevitable because women are not biologically equipped with such an organ. It is largely due to the female's psychological failure to come to terms with the fact she lacks such a 'vital' organ, and her failure to be contented with an 'inferior' clitoris, that results in various forms of mental instability and immaturity. Thus for Freud, psychic pathology and even masculine and feminine personalities are lodged in the bio-sexual realm, and for women biology is seen to be a psychically immature and subordinate destiny frequently attended by trauma and hysteria.

Detailed feminist critiques of Freudian psychoanalytic theories can be found in Mitchell (1974) and Baker Miller (1974) so there is no necessity for such a discussion here. However, it is important to note the significance of the psychoanalytic tradition, for as Gelb states,

Psychoanalysts have contributed to the view of women as weak, inferior, passive ... dependent, unreliable.... Psychoanalysts have tended to lag far behind other workers in the field of human relations in regard to the position of women in our society (Gelb, 1974, p. 367).

Returning to recent empirical sociological studies of women and mental illness, we can examine the work of Gove (1972) and Gove and Tudor (1973) in the USA as attempts to explain why women are more prone to mental breakdown than men. Rather than looking for causes in the biology or psyche of the female sex these studies represent a perspective that looks towards women's roles and status in society as a possible source of conflict and suffering. In Gelb's terms this type of approach has realized that,

much of women's suffering [is] not derived from 'intrapsychic' pathology originating in the early adaptive failure, but that many of their symptoms [are] an ineffectual reaction against their distorted and oppressive sexual-social existence. They could not maintain healthy functioning in such a cruel milieu (Gelb, 1974, pp. 369–70).

In their paper 'Adult Sex Roles and Mental Illness' Gove and Tudor (1973) define mental illness as a disorder which involves personal discomfort and/or mental disorganization that is not caused by an organic or toxic condition, the two diagnostic categories which fit this definition being neurotic disorders and functional psychoses. However, this omits, as they point out, the category 'personality disorders' which is a significant category both in the UK and USA statistics on mental health. Although the diagnosis of 'personality disorder' is statistically evenly distributed between men and women in the UK (with the exception of first admissions where the numbers of men are slightly higher) in the USA there are significantly more men than women apparently suffering from this complaint. Coupled with this Gove and Tudor omit the category of 'alcoholism' which is also a diagnosis most common to men. Having excluded these two categories it can be seen that Gove and Tudor have a tendency in their study to be considering diagnostic categories *known* to be more common statistically amongst women. Bearing this in mind their subsequent results should be treated with some caution.

The proposition that more women than men do suffer from mental illness as defined above is not seriously questioned by Gove and Tudor; instead they take the evidence of a number of studies conducted since the Second World War which indicate that such a proposition is justified. (Unfortunately there is no way of knowing whether these studies use the same definition of mental illness as Gove and Tudor.) This evidence they further attempt to substantiate with statistical data on the numbers and sex of persons being admitted to psychiatric hospitals. They conclude,

In summary, *all* of the information on persons in psychiatric treatment indicates that more women are mentally ill. This information exactly parallels the data from the community studies and is thus consistent with our formulation that the adult woman in modern industrial society is more likely to experience mental illness (Gove and Tudor, 1973, p. 823).

Moreover they claim to have accounted for such possible influences on their findings as societal response and self-selection by looking first at admission figures for mental hospitals (where societal response is considered of prime importance), second at figures for treatment by general practitioners (where self-selection is considered of prime importance) and third at community studies (where selective procedures are considered to be eliminated). In all of these three sections women were found to suffer predominantly from mental illness. A critique of this assumed elimination of 'bias' will be included in the next section but it should be noted here that Gove and Tudor do not specify who the agents of 'societal response' are who commit such large numbers of women to hospital. In other words they omit any discussion of who is in a position not only to define mental illness but to enforce that definition, and also whether these diagnoses are influenced by the double-standard of mental health which applies to women and men. Furthermore, commitment to a mental hospital by a general practitioner cannot be assumed to be a process of self-selection as they suggest, since the doctor's diagnosis and prescribed remedy takes place within a social situation in which hegemonic stereotypical conceptualizations of women are entirely pervasive and in which doctors (of either sex) will perceive their female patients differently from their male patients. Gove and Tudor, in their attempt to eliminate what they perceive as bias by counterbalancing different assessment processes, are in fact adopting the most uncritical, unreflexive techniques of empiricism. From the basic premise that women suffer from mental illness more than men, Gove and Tudor continue to outline what it is about the feminine role, and particularly the married woman's role, that produces such an effect. In his paper 'The Relationship between Sex Roles, Marital Status, and Mental Illness' Gove (1972) found that although more married women than men received treatment for mental illness, more single, divorced and widowed men than similarly situated women received treatment. It would seem therefore that the difference in the rates of mental breakdown between men and women can be entirely accounted for by the numbers of married women suffering from mental illness. This 'finding' provokes Gove into an analysis of the married woman's role but unfortunately he gives little attention to explaining why it is that more single, divorced and widowed men than women apparently suffer from mental breakdowns. Instead he concentrates on the married woman's role in advanced industrialized society, a role which he argues contains five main features likely to lead to mental stress and breakdown. They are as follows:

1 Generally women have only one major social role (that of housewife) and therefore have only one major source of satisfaction. Men on the other hand generally have two major social roles (that of husband/father and breadwinner) and therefore have two sources of satisfaction; if one fails he has an alternative.

2 Many women can be assumed to find their major role frustrat-

ing and of low status especially if it is not commensurate with educational achievements or aspirations.

3 This major role is unstructured and invisible, thus allowing time for 'brooding' and obsession with minor problems.

4 Even when working a (married) woman frequently finds herself in an unsatisfactory position *vis-à-vis* men with similar qualifications. And in addition to working outside the home most women must also work inside it, thereby performing two jobs.

5 Expectations confronting women are often unclear, ambiguous and even contradictory, thus creating a double-bind situation. Traditional roles have lost their value and yet many women are still confined to them, a result of which is low status and low esteem. If these roles are challenged by women however they are likely to be sanctioned negatively.

Certain features of this description of women's roles cannot be disputed, for example discrimination in employment and promotion is a reality for most women. However, Gove and Tudor would appear to be making a vital error in drawing such a sharp dichotomy between men's and women's roles. In contrast Angrist states,

The resultant dichotomies seem to reinforce the clusters of sex-related characteristics: women are women and men are men wherever they may live, eat, play, work or interact.... The issue raised then is the validity of universal sex role behaviour measures without regard to the delineations of other impinging characteristics or to the pertinent social location (Angrist, 1969, p. 217).

In particular such vital factors as socio-economic class, ethnicity and age are overlooked by Gove and Tudor. The possibility of a woman finding satisfaction in work outside the home will depend as much on her socio-economic class as her sex, and although a high incidence of mental breakdown has frequently been correlated with low socio-economic status, Gove does not indicate how this might influence his analysis. Moreover he appears to be saying that if married women stay at home they will become 'broody' and liable to breakdown but if they go out to work they will encounter stress and frustration again making them liable to break-down. This is an assumption which is challenged by Brown *et al.* (1975) in an English study of women of different social classes. Brown *et al.* reveal that going out to work can actually mediate against mental breakdown. They state: 'We have presented evidence that being employed can reduce the chances of developing psychiatric disorder after an event or difficulty even when women lack an intimate tie with husband or boyfriend (Brown *et al.*, 1975, p. 243). The fact that Gove does not consider age or life stage of any importance is also a serious omission. A young married woman who does not go out to work is likely to be at home in order to look after young children. In this case it is most unlikely that her time is unstructured as she does have external demands made upon her; similarly time for 'brooding' will probably be restricted. An older married woman who does not go out to work however is more likely to face the situation Gove describes but once again socio-economic class will be an important factor in determining the nature of the woman's situation.

The crucial question in this discussion is, however, whether the contingencies facing women are in fact more likely to produce mental illness than those facing men. Statistical evidence, particularly relating to married women, suggests that women's traditional role is indeed more likely to produce stress and subsequent breakdown than a man's role. There is therefore a general consensus of opinion, based on such statistical evidence, that women are more prone to mental illness than men. Yet the crux of this discussion, which is not addressed by the studies considered here, is how to interpret statistical evidence and whether to accept such evidence without consideration of the ways in which people come to be defined as mentally ill.

Differential diagnoses and the double-standard of mental health

Before commencing any discussion of the relationship between sex roles, the definition of mental illness and the perceptions of women as held both by 'lay' members of society and the medical profession, it is necessary to examine the categories of mental illness to which most women are assigned. For example, it may be argued that because cultural stereotypes of women portray them to be emotional, irrational, unreliable and immature, psychiatrists and doctors, working within the 'natural attitude', may be more likely to diagnose women as neurotic. Alternatively, because cultural stereotypes of men portray them to be sensible, rational and reliable, a diagnosis of neurosis may be less likely principally because the cause of emotional or irrational behaviour in men will be seen as genuine rather than imaginary or trivial. In other words if one is 'rational' (male) the cause of one's complaint must be real, but if one is 'irrational' (female) the cause of the complaint must be unreal (neurotic). But unless it can be shown that the medical profession does consistently diagnose more women as neurotic than men there can be no substance to this argument. Table 6.3, which shows the rates of admission to psychiatric hospitals and units from the DHSS in-patient statistics, indicates the most common diagnoses for men and women in the years 1970 and 1971. From the data it can be seen that women are most frequently admitted to psychiatric hospitals diagnosed as suffering from the following broad categories. First, schizophrenia, schizo-affective disorders, paranoia; second, depressive psychoses, in-volutional melancholia; third, psychoneuroses; and fourth, a group category known as 'all other conditions'.[2] For men diagnoses of schizophrenia and personality disorders are most common, but only in the category of personality disorders do their numbers equal those of the women. The numbers of men in the UK statistics actually supersede those of women only in the category of alcoholism, which is a small and relatively insignificant diagnostic group when compared with the others shown.

The crucial question is whether these diagnostic rates reflect a situation in which more women than men do actually suffer from mental disorders such as neurosis, or whether a system of differential diagnosis can be said to exist in which different standards or expectations of behaviour are applied to women. Phillips and Segal (1969) argue in support of the latter proposition that '...a person's sexual status affects both the *recognition* and *expression* of illness, and his help-seeking behaviour in response to that illness' (Phillips and Segal, 1969, p. 58). (Emphasis added.)

Table 6.3   *Mental illness hospitals and units under Regional Hospital Boards and Teaching Hospitals*
   Non-first admission rates per 100,000 home population, by diagnostic group and sex (England and Wales)

Diagnostic group	Sex	1970	1971
All diagnoses	M	197	202
	F	273	278
Schizophrenia, schizo-affective disorders, paranoia	M	58	55
	F	61	58
Depressive psychoses, involutional melancholia	M	23	24
	F	55	55
Senile and pre-senile conditions	M	6	6
	F	12	11
Alcoholic psychosis	M	2	3
	F	1	1
Other psychosis	M	10	11
	F	15	16
Psychoneurosis	M	18	18
	F	37	39
Alcoholism	M	14	16
	F	4	4
Drug dependence	M	3	3
	F	2	2
Personality and behaviour disorders	M	22	23
	F	23	23
Mental handicap	M	2	2
	F	2	2
Other psychiatric conditions	M	4	5
	F	5	6
All other conditions*	M	34	36
	F	59	61

Source: *DHSS Inpatient Statistics for Psychiatric Hospitals and Units in England and Wales*, 1970–72.
   * Including depression not specified as neurotic or psychotic, epilepsy, undiagnosed cases and admissions for other than psychiatric disorders.

It has already been argued that the ethic of health is a masculine one (Weisstein, 1971; Chesler, 1974) in which a healthy woman is seen to be synonymous with a 'sick' adult, but Phillips and Segal reach this conclusion from a slightly different route. They argue that the ethic of health is masculine because reward is given to those who bear suffering or pain without making a 'fuss' or without seeking help. While this ethic may not be in accordance with the tenets of preventive medicine; Phillips and Segal argue that it does correspond to the outlook of many harried general practitioners who have little sympathy with what cannot be immediately recognized as 'genuine sickness'. It is because of this ethic that individuals who break the code by complaining too frequently, come to be seen as hypochondriacal or as suffering from some other neurotic ailment. The main point of Phillips and Segal's paper however is that these individuals are most likely to be found among women who, they argue, have a tendency to be 'expressive' about their ailments. The fact that self-report studies on symptoms of physical and mental ill health show that women have higher rates of such symptoms than men does not necessarily mean that women are more frequently disturbed. Rather, it is argued that expressiveness and help-seeking behaviour is a sex-appropriate response for women who are socialized into accepting such a role. Men, on the other hand, are taught to 'grin and bear it' and not to display publicly any kind of suffering or emotional response. Quoting Barker, Phillips and Segal state: 'Particularly among men illness is looked upon as a feminine characteristic to be shunned. The man who publicly announces that he does not know what it means to be sick thereby improves his masculine status' (Phillips and Segal, 1969, p. 60). It would seem therefore that men are more able or willing to conceal or ignore psychological symptoms, thus creating a hidden figure in the official mental health statistics. Women on the other hand will be over-represented because of their willingness to display such symptoms.

This proposition cannot be accepted uncritically however. In their study Phillips and Segal looked only at married men and women which means they have excluded a large section of the population who are affected by mental illness and who, according to Gove (1972), present a very different pattern to that presented by married people. The concept of 'expressiveness' therefore does not account for why single, widowed and divorced men have a slightly higher level of involvement in mental illness than single, widowed and divorced women, nor does it explain why both of these categories fall below the number of married women diagnosed as suffering from mental illness. It may be that 'expressiveness' alone is too simple an explanation and that the low prestige of marital status for women is in fact a contributory factor to mental illness as Gove suggests. However, without further study it is impossible to state whether marriage contributes to greater expressiveness (i.e. once married certain inhibitions with regard to expressiveness are removed) or whether marriage for women is actually more likely to make them suffer from mental illness.

Phillips and Segal have also been criticized by Gove because their suggestion that expressive behaviour by women is socially acceptable would seem to imply that societal response to the expression of their symptoms would be minimal. Put simply, because doctors and psychiatrists 'know' that women complain more about less serious symptoms they will counterbalance this effect by giving them less serious attention. Thus Gove argues implicitly that the statistical data can be seen to be giving a 'true' representation of the differential rates of mental illness for men and women because of this tacit counterbalancing. However, this criticism overlooks the fact that doctors have few other ways of diagnosing psychiatric symptoms other than through the patient's own accounts and cannot know the degree of 'seriousness' independently of the proclaimed suffering of the patient. It may be that doctors and psychiatrists do take their female patients less seriously than their male patients but this cannot merely be assumed when evaluating the statistical evidence. Furthermore, as Chesler maintains, 'The greater social tolerance for female "help-seeking" behaviour, or displays of emotional distress, does not mean that such conditioned behaviour is either valued or treated with kindness' (Chesler, 1974, p. 38). Thus because women are generally socialized into being dependent, expressive beings it does not mean they will escape punishment for having such socially 'undesirable' traits.

The existence of sex-related diagnostic categories is also very important to an understanding of the process whereby people become defined as mentally ill. Neither of the studies discussed above pays any attention to different diagnostic categories and yet the apparent tendency for there to be 'female complaints' and 'male complaints' cannot be ignored. The *DHSS Inpatient Statistics for Psychiatric Hospitals and Units in England and Wales,* 1970–72 (Table 6.3) show that there is a tendency for all types of depressive psychoses, psychoneuroses and non-psychotic, non-neurotic depressions to be predominantly 'female complaints'. On the other hand the typically 'male complaints' are alcoholism and alcoholic psychosis while schizophrenia and personality disorders are complaints to which both sexes seem equally subject. Chesler reports similar findings in the USA although any real comparisons between the USA and the UK data in Tables 6.4 and 6.5 respectively must take account of possible differences in diagnostic criteria which may mean that the diagnostic categories are not exactly comparable.

The main differences between the English and American data appears to be the categories of schizophrenia and personality disorders. In the UK these 'complaints' are equally distributed

Table 6.4 *Percentage incidence of diagnostic classification in General Hospitals in the USA, 1966–8*

Diagnostic classifications	General Hospitals		
	Total no. of patients	% Women	% Men
The 'female diseases'			
Psychotic depressive	30,743	69	31
Manic depressive	28,232	64	36
Psychoneurotic	378,289	70	30
Psychophysiological	27,562	67	33
Psychotic	262,961	64	36
Schizophrenic	158,689	61	39
Paranoid	59,718	57	43
Drug intoxication (poison)	20,229	60	40
The 'male diseases'			
Alcoholic addiction	69,183	25	75
Alcohol intoxication	52,087	27	73
Drug addiction	11,004	36	64
Personality disorders	143,142	40	60

Source: P. Chesler (1974), *Women and Madness,* p. 41.

Table 6.5 *Percentage incidence of diagnostic classification in Psychiatric Hospitals and Units*

Diagnostic group	Total no. of patients	% Male	% Female
Schizophrenia	33,712	48	52
Depressive psychoses	24,855	30·6	69·4
Senile psychoses	10,018	31·5	68·5
Alcoholic psychosis	1,282	74	26
Other psychosis	12,500	40	60
Psychoneurosis	24,839	33	67
Alcoholism	6,705	79	21
Drug dependence	1,593	63	37
Personality and behaviour disorders	16,417	50	50

Source: *DHSS Inpatient Statistics for Psychiatric Hospitals and Units in England and Wales,* 1971.

between the sexes but in the USA the rate of schizophrenia is higher for women while the rate of personality disorders is higher for men. It is interesting to note however that the figures on schizophrenia in State and County hospitals in the USA (as opposed to the General Hospital figures in Table 6.4) are 51 per cent for women and 49 per cent for men. These percentages are very similar to the UK figures in Table 6.5 and it is possible that they are more reliable than those relating to General Hospitals because the State and County Hospitals receive the largest number of diagnosed schizophrenics in the USA (546,237 as opposed to 158,689 for General Hospitals). On the other hand figures for personality disorders in State and County Hospitals are even more disparate than the UK figures (23 per cent of female patients and 77 per cent of male patients diagnosed as suffering from personality disorders) but the total committed to State and County Hospitals with this diagnosis (44,064) is much lower than for the General Hospitals (143,142) so in this case the former figures may be less representative than the latter figures which are shown in Table 6.4.

The statistical 'evidence' for the UK that has been quoted so far has been for psychiatric hospitals and units, and general hospitals. When figures for Special Hospitals[3] (Broadmoor, Rampton and Moss Side) are studied however there appears to be a greater predominance of male patients suffering from schizophrenia and personality disorders than female. It should be noted though that the number of mentally ill in these hospitals is very small in comparison to those in psychiatric or general hospitals (see Table 6.6).

Table 6.6   *Special Hospitals, 1971. Admissions by sex and diagnostic group*

Diagnostic group*	Broadmoor	
	Male	Female
All diagnoses	141	30
Schizophrenia, schizo-affective disorders, paranoia	74	11
Personality and behaviour disorders	34	11
All other conditions	25	4

Diagnostic group*	Rampton		Moss Side	
	Male	Female	Male	Female
All diagnoses	120	46	41	6
Psychoses	12	10	3	—
Neuroses, personality disorders and other non-psychotic mental disorders	74	17	38	6

*Not all the diagnostic groups listed in the DHSS Statistics are listed here.

The addition of figures for Special Hospitals to those for psychiatric and general hospitals makes little difference to the sex ratios of certain diagnostic categories. However, it may be that large numbers of individuals who would be diagnosed as suffering from some form of mental illness, were they presented to a psychiatrist, in fact remain unknown and undiagnosed. This is particularly the case with individuals who perform acts of an anti-social nature (i.e. violence or vandalism) which may imply a personality disorder of some kind to the psychiatrist, but who tend to be counted among the criminal statistics and not the psychiatric data. This is because such individuals, if they are apprehended, are liable to be charged with a criminal offence (not taken to a doctor) and unless they can be proved to be legally insane they will be sent to prison or Borstal rather than a Special Hospital or a psychiatric unit. The distinction between legal and clinical criteria for judging mental health has an important influence on determining who becomes a criminal statistic and who a psychiatric one. Very few male inmates in prisons get psychiatric treatment and those who do are not included in the DHSS mental health statistics and as a result there is no easy way of showing the degree to which criminal and psychiatric cases may overlap. An individual acting in an anti-social way may be defined as mentally ill by doctors but as criminal by the police and courts. Whether or not an act infringes the criminal law is therefore most significant in terms of our understanding of the limitations of official statistics. The degree of threat posed by an individual suffering from mental illness is also instrumental in the process of defining an act as criminal. It seems likely that a man suffering from a personality disorder which manifests itself in anti-social behaviour poses more of a threat to the community or his family than a woman. In which case the men suffering from such disorders may more often be found amongst criminal statistics while the women will become psychiatric statistics. However, it has already been shown that personality disorders are not the most common psychiatric complaint among women, rather they are likely to be defined as schizophrenic, depressive or neurotic. This tendency for the majority of disturbed women to become (or to be diagnosed as) depressed and anxious may be related to the socialization process of girls which encourages them to repress their aggression and to find satisfaction vicariously through others and not on their own initiative. This perhaps has parallels in sex-related criminal activities where women can be seen to adopt deviant behaviour which is most closely related to their traditional feminine roles (i.e. prostitution or shoplifting).

Chesler (1974) presents a similar argument when she states that men are much more likely to reflect a destructive hostility towards others, as well as a pathological self indulgence, while women express self-critical, self-depriving and often self-destructive attitudes. In fact a study of mental hospital patients by Phillips and Zigler in 1960, which is quoted by Chesler, found that males were more likely to 'indulge their impulses in socially deviant ways like "robbery, rape, drinking and homosexuality". Female patients were often found to be "self-deprecatory, depressed, perplexed, suffering from suicidal thoughts or making suicidal attempts"' (Chesler, 1974, p. 39). The problem with this perspective, however, is that it implies that there is a common cause, hinging on a personality disorder, which will result in such behaviour as robbery or rape, depression or suicide depending on which sex is involved. Clearly this is not only too simplistic an analysis but it denies any importance to the different meanings such disparate actions have for the actor. Suicide (cf. Douglas, 1967) is a qualitatively different act to rape, it is not merely abstract violence that can be randomly self- or other-directed. Such actions are also culturally located with specific social meanings such that suicide in a highly individualistic society has a very different social meaning to rape in a society where women are treated as inferior to men and as sexual objects.

To return to the relationship between 'expressiveness' and sex-related diagnostic categories, it can be shown that if these two concepts are combined we have some means of understanding the differential rates of male and female mental breakdown. The diagnostic categories most common to men (i.e. personality disorders and alcoholism) are in the nature of those 'complaints' which tend to be socially visible. In other words, relatives, friends, colleagues and others are likely to become aware of these complaints without the sufferer offering a self-diagnosis or being 'expressive'. Alternatively the diagnostic categories common to women (schizophrenia, depression, neurosis) may not be so socially visible. Others may be unable to recognize that the individual is suffering at all unless she offers a self-diagnosis or is 'expressive'. If this is the case 'expressiveness' is a very significant factor in the diagnosis of certain 'complaints' (i.e. introverted states) but far less important with socially visible 'complaints' (i.e. extra-verted or disruptive states). Thus it is quite possible for men, who are supposedly less expressive than women, to be under-represented in diagnoses of psychoneurosis and depressive psy-choses which require a greater degree of expression for diagnosis but not so with alcoholism and personality disorders. This is undoubtedly a proposition which requires substantiation but I think it might well be a useful avenue of research for explaining diagnostic differences between the sexes.

In the beginning of this section I noted that Phillips and Segal were concerned not only with the expression of illness but also with its recognition. In fact this aspect is hardly dealt with in their paper and yet it is of considerable importance in terms of differen-tial diagnoses. The question is really whether or not a health service which maintains a masculine health ethic is more likely to define women than men as mentally unbalanced (regardless of degrees of expressiveness). I have already pointed to the tradition in psychology which treats women as the most suitable cases for treatment and Chesler (1974) has written in some detail about the patriarchal attitudes of doctors and clinicians towards their female patients. Psychiatric hospital inpatient statistics for England and Wales for 1968–71 show that it is overwhelmingly doctors and psychiatrists who refer individuals to psychiatric hospitals. More-over doctors refer women to these hospitals at a rate of about 50 per 100,000 more than men, and psychiatrists refer them at a rate of 60 per 100,000 more than men. Only the police refer more men than women to psychiatric hospitals; the rate is in fact about double for men. (This rate of referrals of men by the police is probably also indicative of the socially visible nature of the forms of mental breakdown most common among men.) In themselves these figures are not particularly informative but a study by Linn (1961) of the agents involved in hospitalization does reveal the way in which sexual status plays an important part in who is hospitalized and by whom. Linn's study was carried out between 1953–6 in the district of Columbia, USA. It was found that with married patients it was overwhelmingly the spouse who arranged for commitment and it was more likely to be the husband than the wife. Spouses arranged for the commitment of 55 per cent of white males but 69 per cent of white females and in the Negro community spouses had committed 43 per cent of Negro males but 73 per cent of Negro females. With unmarried individuals it was the parents or sibling who arranged commitment, but once again far more were arranged on the behalf of women (i.e. 50 per cent of white males, 79 per cent of white females, 50 per cent of Negro males and 71 per cent of Negro females). Linn argues that these differential rates can be explained in terms of a responsibility (or authority) structure. This responsibility (or authority) manifests itself according to a perceived right to 'interfere' in the lives of others. Thus parents have a right to interfere in the lives of their children, a right which decreases as the child's age increases. However, because of the inferior status of women both husbands and parents perceive themselves to have a right to 'interfere' in their lives regardless, as Linn discovered, of age or whether the women were economically independent or not. Linn also found that the closer the family relations the lower the tolerance rate for deviant behaviour and this finding may be an important factor in accounting for Gove's argument that more married women than single are diagnosed as suffering from mental illness.[4] The role of relatives in committing individuals to hospital is still an unknown factor in the UK, as is their role in persuading them to go to a doctor or psychiatrist in the first place. Linn's study suggests that husbands are vitally instrumental in the case of married women but this needs further confirmation by similar studies in the UK.

One other point arising from Linn's study was that women are far less likely to be tolerated by their husbands if their deviance takes a form not usually associated with the feminine role, in other words if they become violent or fail to function as a woman 'should'. This role rejection leading to hospitalization appears to be a contradiction to an earlier argument which implied that conformity to the feminine role of itself can be defined as 'sick' and in need of treatment. Yet both of these two modes of behaviour can in fact be defined as symptomatic of illness, as Chesler states: 'What we consider "madness" whether it appears in women or in men is either the acting-out of the devalued *female* role or the total or partial rejection of one's sex-role stereotype' (Chesler,

1974, p. 53). (Emphasis added.) Thus women would appear to be in a double-bind situation where acceptance of the stereotypical feminine role has derogatory effects and the rejection of the same role also results in negative sanctions.

In concluding this section it is important to recognize that none of the studies discussed above have addressed the question of the socio-economic class of women suffering from mental illness. Class however can be an influential factor in several ways. If the health service is indeed a paternalistic one operating with hegemonic conceptions of women, working-class women may be more vulnerable than middle-class women in the diagnostic situation. In his paper 'Individual Resources, Societal Reaction and Hospital Commitment', Rushing (1971) argues that socio-economic status as well as marital status are important contingencies in societal reaction. In particular he argues that the ability to sue for wrongful admission to a mental hospital means that those of higher socio-economic status will have greater protection from the administration of such treatment. On the other hand although socio-economic status may be important in terms of diagnosis and treatment of mental illness (in the way it appears to be with the definition and treatment of criminal behaviour) there may also be a strong case for arguing that the low status of women in general combined with low socio-economic status may make some women more vulnerable not only to a differential diagnosis of mental breakdown but also to mental breakdown itself. Brown *et al.* (1975) have studied a group of women in the community, as opposed to psychiatric in-patients or out-patients, to discover what factors are related to mental disturbance. Those they defined as disturbed were women who expressed symptoms similar in type and extent to those usually considered in need of treatment by psychiatrists. However, this definition neglects the question of whether one should accept uncritically the criteria used by psychiatrists in assessing mental health, and its usage is therefore subject to the same criticism as that levelled at criminological studies which accept the legal (official) definition of crime. Brown *et al.* do partially defend themselves from such criticism however by arguing that the disturbance they discovered amongst their sample was inherently unpleasant. They state: 'When, as in depressive disorders, distress-anguish is associated with complaints such as early-morning wakening, lack of energy, feelings of worthlessness and so on, and they persist for months on end, the experience becomes scarcely endurable' (Brown *et al.*, 1975, p. 226).

Working within this definition of mental breakdown, Brown *et al.* discovered that working-class women were more vulnerable to mental distress because of a combination of stressful life events (i.e. threatened evictions) and difficult periods in their marriages. They discovered that the relationship between working-class spouses deteriorated after the birth of the first child and did not improve until all the children were growing up, but this pattern was not evident with middle-class marriages. Consequently, if intimacy between husband and wife is at a low ebb at a time when threatening life events occur, young married working-class women are likely to be the most vulnerable to mental illness. Other significant features contributing to greater vulnerability were found to be, first, the loss of the woman's mother by death or separation before the age of eleven, second, having three or more children aged fourteen or less at home, and third, the lack of full- or part-time employment. But these factors were only important in combination with threatening life events. Although the second and third factors are related to life stage, Brown *et al.* also found that the number of children and the loss of the woman's mother were factors related to class as well, thus contributing to the greater vulnerability of working-class women.

In conclusion it would appear that the perceived higher rate of mental illness for women than men cannot simply be accounted for by an inherent bias against women in a masculine health ethos adopted by the health services. Nevertheless consideration must be given to hegemonic stereotyped conceptions of women which may be able to account for the over-representation of women in statistical evidence. Yet the fact that women's stereotyped traditional role, which limits her economic independence and isolates her in the home with only childrearing and domestic duties as sources of fulfilment, is still a distressing reality for many women cannot be denied. To argue that the excessive numbers of women who suffer from mental breakdown is due only to the process of defining mental illness is to underestimate the low status and unsatisfactory nature of women's position in advanced industrial society. Both Gove and Tudor (1973) and Brown *et al.* (1975) relate vulnerability to mental illness to social factors. To this extent their work is critical of the structure of society which places so many women in such untenable circumstances. However, they overlook the fact that the majority of agents concerned with defining and diagnosing mental illness (or indeed any deviant behaviour) are concerned more with 'normalizing' behaviour than radically altering the inequitable structure of society. Thus they concentrate on vulnerability in terms of life events and status and not in terms of a powerlessness to deflect or reject such definitions of behaviour as mental illness or deviance. For this reason their work is inadequate if treated as a total explanation of the incidence of mental illness amongst women. A more satisfactory explanation has to include an understanding of both kinds of vulnerability, vulnerability to low status and stressful life events and vulnerability to a detrimental labelling process.

Mental illness as a functional equivalent to crime

Statistical evidence showing that men commit more crime than women and conversely that women are more vulnerable to mental breakdown than men provides a basis for the view that mental illness is for women a functional equivalent to crime. It has already been shown, however, that statistical evidence is unreliable as a basis for theoretical understanding. Yet in spite of the unreliable nature of official statistics there is another foundation for the 'functional equivalence' thesis, namely that differential opportunity structures and socialization processes will lead men and women to dissimilar actions when faced with similar problems or situations. Thus it can be argued that the normative restraint experienced by most women orients them towards being non-aggressive, caring, unambitious and so on. Consequently, the argument continues, there will be a tendency for women to become introverted and self-destructive if they deviate. In contrast the socialization of males encourages them to be aggressive, assertive and outward-going with the result that they are likely to become violent or anti-social in a criminal fashion if they deviate. This neat division between the sexes is somewhat unrealistic, however, because it ignores the fact that not all members of society accept uncritically their socially assigned gender roles. Not all men are aggressive or potentially violent and not all women are passive and caring, although it is often still expected that men and women should display the appropriate characteristics. Moreover, women who do turn to crime and men who suffer from mental illness represent a considerable problem for such an analysis.

A more significant criticism of this functional equivalence thesis is the assumption on which it is founded, that the social meaning of different forms of deviance is of no consequence. Becoming neurotic, for example, is a qualitatively different act from robbing or assaulting a person. It has a different meaning and consequence for both the actor and others who may be involved. Criminality and mental illness cannot be said to have a common cause, cannot be said to be merely different modes of expression which are appropriate to the different sexes, unless, that is, both phenomena are treated as occurring in a social vacuum and all forms of deviance are held to be mutually interchangeable. The assumption within the 'functional equivalence' thesis is that the specific form of deviance is virtually meaningless, what is considered as significant is the function or need it fulfils.

Equating crime and mental illness in this way can clearly have serious implications for policy decision which concern female offenders because, if mental illness is seen as the appropriate deviant 'outlet' for women, committing crimes becomes merely an extension of a presumed mental instability or illness. Consequently all forms of deviant behaviour in women can be assumed to be irrational, illogical and unintentional. The functional equivalence thesis, by treating mental illness as the appropriate form of deviance for women and by reducing the significance of the social meanings of different forms of deviance, ultimately treats female criminality as an outcome of mental instability.

Yet this outcome is not inevitable. Only if mental illness is assumed to be irrational and illogical behaviour can criminality, by association, be treated similarly. If mental illness is perceived of as rational, meaningful behaviour, then mental illness and criminal behaviour need not be seen as functional equivalents but as categories of action which are explicable in terms of the meaning and intentions of the actor. For example, it may be possible to perceive of certain types of mental illness as a rational and logical outcome of irrational and untenable social circumstances (cf. Laing and Esterson, 1970). Or as Shoham (1974) has argued, schizophrenia in particular can be explained by a learning process coupled with the effects of labelling (cf. Scheff, 1974). Shoham's argument is that schizophrenia is a culturally transmitted type of behaviour which is learnt through a process of differential association in a way that is comparable to criminal behaviour (Sutherland and Cressey, 1966). Shoham, like Laing and Sutherland, argues that the family is the greatest source of influence due to the intimacy and length of contact between members. Once definitions favourable to deviant action are learnt he maintains that the labelling process is of vital importance as it confirms the individual in his or her deviant career. Shoham maintains that the labelling and stigmatizing processes in mental institutions prevent any 'remedy' and confirm deviant identity in the same way that prisons 'create' hardened criminals and recidivists. We can observe therefore that some forms of mental illness may be explained in ways similar to criminal behaviour without having to resort to biological, physiological or psychic causes in which the actor is seen as the mere recipient of impulses. It should be remembered, however, that crime and mental illness can only be treated as similar if it is allowed that a career in insanity has meaning and reason for the actor. If this controversial premise is not accepted, then equating crime with insanity may have very serious consequences for both our understanding of deviance and the treatment of offenders, particularly female offenders.

Conclusion

In this chapter I have considered the changing relationship between crime and mental illness and in particular how this has affected women. The neglect of a serious scientific analysis of women's involvement in crime in criminological studies has been paralleled by a considerable interest in women by psychologists and others who have attempted to analyse women's 'vulnerability' to mental illness. As a result crime has become seen as male deviation and mental disturbance has come to be associated with female deviation. Such a division, however, is arbitrary and reduces rather than clarifies our understanding of these social phenomena. Given this crude division of labour between the sexes it becomes difficult to account for female criminality and male insanity. That the structure of society may present men with more opportunity and predisposition to become criminal and women with more opportunity and predisposition to become mentally ill is not fundamentally disputed here. What is disputed is that these opportunities and predispositions are inherent in the nature of men and women. Moreover I have attempted to illustrate the significance of the process by which women (and by omission, men) become defined as mentally ill. In partial agreement with Coulter (1973) I suggest that 'The sociologist must turn away from "explanation" of the whys of insanity and towards a description of the hows of insanity *ascription*' (Coulter, 1973, p. 113). Certainly such an approach is revealing of the basic assumptions which underlie the common belief that women are more 'prone' to mental illness than men.

Chapter 7

Redressing the balance: Women and criminology

It is not correct to state that women have been entirely ignored in the study of crime and deviance. Women do constitute a topic in the existing criminological literature; however, the quality of the work which does address the question of female criminality leaves much to be desired. Studies which make some kind of reference to women may be divided into two categories, namely those which make an explicit reference to female criminality and those in which the topic is left implicit. I have dealt with studies which refer explicitly to female criminality in some detail. The limitations of the majority of these studies arise as a result of a basic inadequacy in the perception of the nature of women and a reliance upon a determinate model of female behaviour. Such studies (cf. Lombroso and Ferrero, 1895; Cowie, Cowie and Slater, 1968) presume an inherent and 'natural' distinction exists between the temperament, ability and conditionability of women and men and recourse is made to this premise to explain female criminality. Other studies (cf. Pollak, 1961) perpetuate the myth of the evil woman whose physiology is the source of her ability to deceive and manipulate, whilst work also exists (cf. Greenwald, 1958; Gibbens, 1957; Glover, 1969) which draws upon the 'feminine psyche' to account for female criminality under the assumption that any rejection of the traditional female role, as in criminal behaviour, is indicative of a personality disorder. The essence of all these studies is that women are treated as fundamentally and qualitatively different from men. Of course there are differences but those differences which exist and which are relevant to an understanding of criminal behaviour are culturally determinate rather than a reflection of the *natural* qualities of the sexes. This type of analysis of female offenders is not peculiar to male criminologists; incredibly even those studies which are written, or partially written, by women (cf. Cowie *et al.*, 1968; Richardson, 1969) contain derogatory and sexist attitudes about women. Unfortunately this tendency for women sociologists and criminologists to support the prevailing, male-oriented ideology merely serves to perpetuate that ideology and even lends it greater credibility.

The second category of criminological study includes those studies which refer only implicitly to female offenders or which refer to them indirectly in token recognition. For example, in the latter category can be included Walker's *Crime and Punishment in Britain* (1973) and Hall-Williams's *The English Penal System in Transition* (1970). In both of these studies women are allocated a minor reference; they are categorized alongside juvenile delinquents and mentally abnormal offenders—a classification no doubt symbolic of women's traditional civil and legal status, that is, comparable to children and 'lunatics'. In many criminological studies female offenders are not mentioned at all, either their very existence is ignored or they are held to be too insignificant to be worthy of consideration. The deviant, the criminal or the actor is always male; it is always *his* rationality, *his* motivation, *his* alienation, or *his* victim. And this is more than a convenient choice of words; the selection of the male pronoun may be said to be inclusive of the female but in reality it is not; it merely excludes women and makes them invisible. Moreover the assumption that the male includes the female is not a very satisfactory argument; it does not allow an equal weighting or consideration for both sexes. On the contrary the female is subsumed by the male, her experience of the world is never expressed even though it may be and frequently is different from the male experience. Essentially the woman is not given a voice because it is assumed the man can speak for her. As de Beauvoir maintains,

This humanity is male and man defines woman not in herself but as relative to him; she is not regarded as an autonomous being.... She is defined and differentiated with reference to man and not he with reference to her; she is the incidental, the inessential as opposed to the essential. He is the Subject, he is the Absolute—she is the Other (de Beauvoir, 1974, p. 16).

It is no surprise that our language and choice of words reflects the social 'invisibility' of women because in our culture, man is the centre of the universe and woman features only in her relation to him. Consequently within criminology we have studies of male criminals and male juvenile delinquents. Where are the women? Generally women are the wives or mothers of these men or boys. Women are the ones who are believed to cause their men to act, usually through manipulation, but it is the men who act. Mothers are held to be responsible for the delinquency of their children but it is the feelings and actions of the children that are studied. In each case women are in the shadows; they prepare the scene for their men and children to act but they do not warrant consideration themselves. In spite of claims to the contrary therefore, the innumerable studies of criminality and delinquency that exist do not include women and girls in their subject-matter. They are written largely by men, on the subject of men for an audience of men. Take, for example, the following quotation: 'This book is therefore about how theories are developed (by men), how they are read and received (by men), and how they might be implemented in action (by men)' (Pearson, 1975, p. x). The accuracy of this statement is beyond question, women *are* excluded from the processes described and yet the exclusion of women by the author was probably unintentional—so much is it taken for granted that women are insignificant members of our community.

The problem that is posed by implicit and explicit references to women in the social sciences is how to proceed from here to deal with the subject of women. Clearly this is a strange question to have to pose, especially when referring to a sector of the community which constitutes more than half of its members. And yet the question remains, do we talk of, and study women separately from men so that we have a sociology or criminology or psychology of women, or do we study men and women together? If we take the former course there are both advantages and disadvantages. Primarily it would be advantageous to make women 'visible' in the social sciences and to institute research projects that would really be concerned with the world and interests of women. But in so doing there is a risk of creating what might be called a 'ghetto' effect, that is to say, women's studies might become segregated from the mainstream of the social sciences and classified as 'women's work'. In other words, women would be encouraged to study women and the whole area would be considered low in status and receive little support from the existing male-dominated community of social scientists. On the other hand, a possible and even worse outcome is that male or male-oriented social scientists, who have little commitment to feminism, might appropriate this 'new' area of study, treating it analytically in ways similar to any other subject of study. In this case the topic of women and crime would become yet another area in social science, like education, industry or race, to be added to the existing list of subjects studied, leaving basic sexist attitudes inherent in the social sciences undisturbed. As Smith argues,

it is not enough to supplement an established sociology by addressing ourselves to what has been left out, overlooked, or by making sociological issues of the relevances of the world of women. That merely extends the authority of the existing sociological procedures and makes of a woman's sociology an addendum (Smith, 1973, p. 7).

The appropriation of this 'new' area of study as Smith describes it has already begun and there is a danger that it will be subsumed into the prevailing sociological paradigm in the way that even functionalism can absorb Marxism or empiricism can accommodate ethnomethodology.

An alternative to the 'separatist' approach does not yet exist. Ultimately a non-separatist social science must be the desired goal because women and men do not act separately in the social world, they are not independent of each other and their inter-relationship is a vital fact of life. But before this goal can be achieved changes in ideology and social practices must take place, and woman must no longer be treated as the 'inessential'; the negative to man's positive. In order to achieve such a transformation basic changes in consciousness are necessary and it is here, through consciousness raising that separate studies of women and the concerns of women, by feminists, are vital. The aim must be not only to make visible the invisible, to restore women in their own right to social science, but to find alternative modes of conceptualizing the social world so that the interests and concerns of women are addressed and included rather than subsumed or ignored.

Women: the unrecognized victims

Women are not only invisible actors in the criminological literature; they also constitute an absence as victims. They are the unrecognized victims not only of criminal acts and enterprises (such as rape and prostitution) but also of the criminal law, penal policy and criminological theories. As victims of criminal behaviour, battered wives and women seeking abortions can be included alongside rape victims and prostitutes. In each of these cases women may be the victims of individuals or organizations or simply the law and yet they are rarely perceived as such. With wife-battering the victim is often in a position similar to that of the rape victim. It is generally assumed that a woman who is beaten by a man in some way 'deserves' her punishment in the way that the rape victim 'deserves' or 'asks' to be raped. The concept of victim-precipitation is therefore employed to make the victim appear responsible for her own demise, thereby rendering the victims of such offences non-existent (cf. Select Committee on Violence in Marriage, 1975). Even the actual occurrence of wife-beating and rape has been largely ignored in criminological literature until very recently. This is perhaps because women have been reticent to complain about the assaults they have suffered, knowing quite well they would receive little sympathy or help from the police or legal system, but as both offences are well known to occur with some frequency the silence of criminologists on this subject is strange indeed. One cannot help wondering whether the victims of these offences being women has influenced the criminologist's or sociologist's interest, especially where the majority are male.

The woman seeking an abortion is no longer such an obvious victim as she was before the implementation of the 1967 Abortion Act. Before abortions on the grounds of 'social reasons' were legally permissible, a pregnant woman who did not want a child had little choice other than an illegal abortion or having the baby. No other recourse was open to her unless it could be shown on medical grounds that the birth would threaten her life. This law was operative at a time when knowledge about contraceptive methods was not widely disseminated and when the most reliable forms of contraception were not as freely or easily available as they are now (cf. Schofield, 1975). In such a situation it was inevitable that women would become pregnant against their wishes and would be unable to find a legitimate solution. In effect therefore many women were victims of government policy and the criminal law, for those who had their babies, but did not want them, suffered, whilst those who had illegal abortions ran the risk of serious infection and a criminal charge. A large number of women therefore must have committed a criminal offence before 1967 and yet they appear nowhere in the traditional criminological literature, either as offenders or as the victims of policies which denied women the right to determine their own bodies and lives. This 'woman's' problem has remained beyond the realms of interest of criminology.

An additional silence exists in the criminological literature on the effect of the imprisonment of men on their families. Most studies are concerned with the etiology of crime and delinquency or with the effects of penal policy on offenders; rarely are they concerned with the other aspects of crime which might be most significant for women. For example little consideration is given to the impact on women of having their men put in prison. The hardship suffered by a woman, and possibly her children, through losing her man and living on social security if she is unable to work rarely features in studies on the effects of imprisonment. In studies such as *Psychological Survival* by Taylor and Cohen (1972) we learn of the anguish suffered by the imprisoned men who are separated from their families but we hear nothing of the suffering of the women and their families who are the other side of that relationship. Here again women are treated as marginal to what are defined as the central and important issues even though the effects of imprisonment may be as hard and punitive for women outside prison as for their menfolk inside.

Finally, women may be said to suffer another unrecognized injustice where they are the direct objects of penal policy. This follows from the reinforcement of the typical feminine role in women and girls who are in penal or local authority institutions. Such policies are geared to supporting the inferior position of women in society in the naïve belief that femininity is the antithesis of criminality. The assumption that the liberation of women will lead to more female criminality receives a great deal of support from criminologists who are critical of the Women's Movement for its disturbing effects on women (cf. Berry, 1974; Hart, 1975). We can see therefore that a consensus of opinion exists which serves in practice to encourage women to remain in their traditional domestic roles whilst implicitly discouraging a questioning of women's social position and status. This deliberate reinforcement of the traditional feminine model produces a situation in which the female offender becomes not only disadvantaged through spending time in an institution and possibly acquiring a record of criminal or delinquent behaviour but also through having her socially inferior status confirmed. With the introduction of anti-discrimination legislation such injustices may eventually disappear, but until such discrimination is made obvious and visible there is little hope that progress will occur.

Prospects and possibilities

At this conjuncture the formulation of an alternative perspective, perhaps a feminist criminology to take its place alongside the ranks of New, Critical, Radical and Working-Class Criminologies, might appear desirable. Indeed a feminist criminology is significantly absent from the above list for it is quite clear that these criminologies do not include a feminist perspective or even a more serious consideration of female offenders than the traditional 'old' criminologies. Consequently, because the new criminologies fail to address the question of women it might seem that we should ourselves formulate a feminist criminology, or perhaps more appropriately a feminist sociology (since criminology has invested so much of its interest in social policy and control). Or *should* we be drawn, at this premature stage, into attempting to succeed in a search for alternatives where so many have failed before. As Firestone maintains,

The classic trap for any revolutionary is always, 'What's your alternative?' But even if you *could* provide the interrogator with a blueprint, this does not mean he would use it: in most cases he is not sincere in wanting to know.... Moreover, the oppressed have no job to convince all people. All *they* need know is that the present system is destroying them (Firestone, 1973, pp. 210–11).

Any alternative perspective I might offer here is bound to be unsatisfactory because it is not adequate to present a theory which is based solely on the negation of existing theories. In the movement towards developing a feminist perspective a critique of sexism is vital, but in itself a critique alone cannot constitute a new theoretical approach. Further work is necessary in criminology and sociology before the desired goal of a women's perspective can be achieved (cf. Smith, 1973). In particular more research is needed in the area of women and crime because there is a dearth of material which even considers women, let alone analyses their deviant and criminal behaviour in non-sexist terms. I am aware that such a request for more research may produce a hostile and derisive response. For example, consider Pearson's attitude towards conclusions of this kind. He states,

That kind of conclusion should be recognised for what it is: a way of dodging the problem of arriving at a conclusion.... Also, as a way of ending—or abandoning—a study, an appeal for more research begs another question: research for what? There is no shortage of research on deviance (Pearson, 1975, p. x).

Although Pearson's comment may be considered appropriate for the field of male criminality and deviance, it has little relevance for the question of criminality and deviance involving women other than to confirm the existence of a total lack of awareness of the neglect of female criminality in both 'old' and 'new' criminologies. Even the well-trod paths of subcultural theory have failed to reveal much interest in the membership of girls in gangs and subcultures (cf. McRobbie and Garber, 1975). Clearly there *is* a requirement for more research, including a re-appraisal and a re-interpretation of existing material in terms of our reconceptualization of the role of women and girls in the community.

There are many specific areas in which research is necessary; the most obvious are as follows:

1 The types of offences committed by women and girls and the form that their involvement in criminality and delinquency takes. For a long time it has been assumed that women commit only 'feminine' offences (i.e. shoplifting or sexual deviance) and that their involvement in crime or gangs and subcultures is essentially passive. But these assumptions may well be more a reflection of the perceptions of male researchers relying on their contact with male sub-cultures than an accurate reflection of the activities of women and girls.

2 Police, probation officers' and social workers' attitudes towards delinquent girls and criminal or deviant women. It has been assumed that a benevolent attitude is adopted by these agencies but as more critical analyses are being completed both in the UK and the USA it has become apparent that this benevolence has been exaggerated.

3 The treatment of women and girls in Crown, Magistrates' and Juvenile Courts. In addition to looking at the social interaction between judges, barristers, defendants and complainants, attention needs to be given to the question of whether women actually do receive more lenient sentences than men. What is required here is a comparative analysis of the sentences received by female and male offenders in terms of both the type of offence committed and previous criminal record.

4 The treatment of female offenders in prisons, Borstals, remand centres, community homes and any other penal or quasi-penal institution. There is sufficient research on inmate relationships but what is lacking is an analysis of the policies of individual institutions, especially as they relate to the perpetuation of traditional female roles.

5 The structure and purposes of criminal laws. Officially it is stated that the criminal law treats both sexes equally; it now seems appropriate to analyse this assumption.

There are undoubtedly other areas of research that I have not mentioned which are possibly of equal importance to the above. The point is, however, not to present an exhaustive list but merely to indicate the existing silences and absences in the hope that the relevant topics and issues will eventually be addressed.

Finally it is important that future studies of female criminality are situated in the wider moral, political, economic and sexual spheres which influence women's status and position in society. An isolated study of court-room procedure or police attitudes to female offenders would be meaningless without an analysis of attitudes towards women in general; for example, whether they are thought to be more deceitful than men; whether their sexuality is treated differently from male sexuality, or whether a woman's economic dependence is taken for granted. The origins of beliefs, attitudes and practices which may be shared by social control agencies and female offenders need to be explored and integrated into the study of female criminality. In the past these factors have remained implicit or have even been used uncritically as 'evidence' to confirm the natural and inevitable qualities of the existing social order; it is now necessary to question these assumptions. The initial aims for analysis are therefore modest, namely to reveal and account for the existing social practices within the legal and penal systems. By attending to the question of female criminality and deviance our understanding of existing social practices within the legal and penal systems will be enhanced and it may then be possible to move towards the formulation of proposals for radically reforming our system of justice. Criminology and the sociology of deviance must become more than the study of men and crime if it is to play any significant part in the development of our understanding of crime, law and the criminal process and play any role in the transformation of existing social practices.

Statistics on rape from 1969 to 1974

Table AI.1   *Persons (male) proceeded against for rape offences and the result of proceedings. Magistrates' Courts (all ages)*

	1969	1970	1971	1972	1973	1974
Total no. proceeded against (x)	468	467	437	508	501	538
Proceedings discontinued	—	—	—	—	6	3
Discharged	21	16	6	7	6	13
Committed for trial at Crown Courts (y):						
a) in custody	163	165	153	154	162	180
b) on bail	250	252	245	307	297	308
Charge withdrawn or dismissed	8	18	15	14	16	10
Total dealt with at Magistrates' level only (x−y)	55	50	39	47	42	50
Total found guilty	24	13	14	20	14	24

Sentences						
Absolute discharge	—	—	—	—	—	—
Recognizance	—	—	—	—	—	—
Conditional discharge	4	—	1	1	—	6
Hospital Order S.60 Mental Health Act 1959	—	—	1	—	—	—
Probation	4	7	—	—	—	—
Supervision (previously Fit Person) Order	—	—	8	6	1	3
Fine	3	1	—	3	4	2
Attendance Centre	—	1	—	—	—	4
Detention Centre	6	1	2	—	6	2
Care (previously approved school)	5	3	1	3	2	5
Suspended sentence	—	—	—	—	2	—
Imprisonment	2	—	—	—	—	—

	1969	1970	1971	1972	1973	1974
Committed for sentence at Crown Court	—	—	1	7	1	2
Proceedings not completed	2	3	4	6	—	—

Table AI.2 *Persons (male) for trial for rape offences and the result of proceedings. Crown Courts (formerly Assizes and Quarter Sessions) (all ages)*

	1969	1970	1971	1972	1973	1974
Total number for trial	294	359	357	358	429	410
Not tried:						
a) No prosecution	—	—	—	—	2	2
b) Unfit to plead	—	—	1	—	2	1
Acquitted	89	68	102	98	111	90
Not guilty by reason of insanity	1	—	—	—	—	—
Total found guilty	204	291	254	260	314	317
Sentences						
Absolute discharge	—	—	—	2	—	—
Recognizance	—	—	—	1	1	—
Conditional discharge	2	2	6	2	—	5
Hospital Order S.60 Mental Health Act 1959	2	2	1	—	1	2
Restriction Order S.65 Mental Health Act 1959	8	11	3	6	9	6
Probation	4	6	11	5	9	8
Supervision	N/A	N/A	—	—	1	1
Fine	3	5	2	6	4	1
Detention Centre	8	12	8	9	12	8
Care (formerly approved school)	1	2	3	—	—	—
Borstal training	29	47	22	27	42	45
Returned to Borstal	—	—	1	—	—	—
Suspended sentence	9	13	18	14	17	14
Imprisonment (immediate)	135	186	178	188	216	224
Extended sentence	1	2	1	N/A	N/A	N/A
Otherwise dealt with	2	3	—	—	2	3

Source: *Home Office Statistics for England and Wales*, 1969 to 1974; Tables Ia and IIa.

Statistics on assault from 1969 to 1974

Table AII.1   *Persons (male) proceeded against for assault. Magistrates' Courts (all ages)*

	1969	*1970*	*1971*	*1972*	*1973*	*1974*
Total no. proceeded against (x)	234	260	258	274	343	370
Proceedings discontinued	N/A	N/A	N/A	N/A	5	3
Discharged	—	—	—	—	1	1
Committed for trial at Crown Courts (y):						
a) in custody	—	4	5	6	5	1
b) on bail	10	28	19	16	27	16
Charge withdrawn or dismissed	26	22	29	22	30	63
Total dealt with at Magistrates' level only ($x - y$)	224	228	234	252	311	353
Total found guilty	188	199	197	222	275	286

Table AII.2   *Persons (male) for trial for assault. Crown Courts (formerly Assizes and Quarter Sessions) (all ages)*

	1969	1970	1971	1972	1973	1974
Total number for trial*	193	245	302	303	365	365
Not tried:						
a) No prosecution	—	1	1	—	1	2
b) Unfit to plead	—	—	—	—	—	1
Acquitted	4	8	8	4	5	21
Not guilty by reason of insanity	—	—	—	—	—	—
Total found guilty	189	236	293	299	359	341

* Although very few people are sent from Magistrates' Courts to Crown Courts for trial for assault a substantial number are nonetheless tried by jury. This is because after commitment for trial large numbers of defendants will have the charge against them altered, usually lessened, if they agree to plead guilty. It is therefore likely that a number of people originally charged with more serious offences such as malicious wounding or grievous bodily harm will actually be tried for a lesser offence like assault if they agree to plead guilty.

Table AII.3   *Offences (assault) recorded as known to the police*

Year	Number of assaults known to police
1969	566
1970	531
1971	551
1972	920
1973	879
1974	1,138

Source: *Home Office Statistics for England and Wales*, 1969 to 1974; Tables Ia, IIa and 1.

Notes

Chapter 1   The nature of female criminality

1 See chapter 5 for a full discussion of the possible social implications of present conceptions and theories of female criminality.
2 Whether the exclusion of men from the offence category of infanticide is in fact a case of discrimination against men is debatable. Certainly infanticide is an offence which is looked upon more leniently than child destruction or murder but unfortunately men do not have the opportunity of claiming that the trauma of birth affects them also. This is because the psychological disturbance that women suffer after childbirth is seen as mainly physiologically (hormonally) induced rather than culturally produced. Should this post-natal psychological disturbance be understood as a consequence of the shock of parenthood and the parents' perception of a totally changed life-style it might be feasible to argue that both parents are vulnerable to psychological disturbances of this kind.
3 There is of course a strong element of sexual discrimination in a law which attempts to punish male homosexuality in certain circumstances while ignoring female homosexuality completely.
4 Similar legal definitions of prostitution exist in the UK too, for example the definition given by Lord Parker, C.J. in Webb (1964): 'prostitution is proved if it be shown that a woman offers her body for purposes amounting to common lewdness for payment in return' (Smith and Hogan, 1973, p. 344). It should be noted, however, that it is not an offence to be a prostitute but only to solicit or to run a brothel.
5 For a fuller exposition of this controversial statement see chapter 5.
6 Since the 1967 Abortion Act and the legalization of abortion under certain conditions (cf. Ashdown-Sharp, 1975) the numbers of men and women involved in procuring illegal abortions is likely to have declined, although while abortion is not freely or easily available there

will always be women who have to resort to unsafe, non-medical means of abortion. Prior to 1970 the official criminal statistics referred only to 'procuring abortion' as an offence; since 1970 this categorization has been modified to read 'procuring illegal abortion'. Significantly since the 1967 Act abortion has become an area of much greater concern to men because the majority of our doctors both in the NHS and in private practice are male.

7 It should be noted that Morris's study is not without major methodological limitations. In testing attitudes towards delinquency the boys and girls in the sample were asked different questions, although the questions were said to be of equivalent relevance for eliciting information about attitudes to deviance. For example the boys were asked how they felt about violence or car theft while the girls were asked about promiscuous sexual relations and heavy petting. Morris argues that the purpose of these different questions was to test the double-standard of morality, but as the boys and girls were not asked the same questions, and as it was assumed that sexual behaviour would have a different significance for both sexes on an *a priori* basis, it can only be concluded that Morris actually imposed the double-standard before the test began.

8 For example the 1957 Wolfenden Committee on Homosexual Offences and Prostitution resulted in the 1959 Street Offences Act which made streetwalking and soliciting by female prostitutes an offence. This had the result of removing most prostitutes from the streets so that prostitution became far less visible and less easy to detect. Moreover the implementation of the Act has meant that, as long as prostitutes do not solicit illegally and do not live in brothels or with other prostitutes, they can remain undetected by the police. This of course has led to an even greater disparity between classes of prostitutes, as high-class prostitutes and call girls can remain relatively immune from arrest while ordinary prostitutes who have to streetwalk not only earn less but are more likely to be arrested, fined and even imprisoned.

Chapter 2 *Classical studies of female criminality*

1 How this concept has developed will be considered in later chapters. It can be noted briefly here that it has been transformed from a biological to a psychological and psychoanalytical concept in later studies. For example, Pollak sees the prone and inactive position of women during sexual intercourse as producing particular attitudes towards deceit. Psychoanalytic studies (i.e. Fromm, quoted in Baker Miller, 1974) have similarly assumed that the passive role in sexual

intercourse which is 'naturally' taken by women is symbolic of the passive nature of true femininity and a sign of normal adjustment.

2 Lombroso goes so far as to quote Euripides to prove his point: 'The violence of the ocean waves or of devouring flame is terrible. Terrible is poverty, but woman is more terrible than all else'; and an Italian proverb: 'Rarely is a woman wicked, but when she is she surpasses the man.'

3 Garfinkel's (1967) study of Agnes is revealing of the learnt and achieved nature of gender roles and provides strong evidence against those who maintain that both sex and gender are ascribed.

4 'Freely' is used here as a relative and culturally located concept and does not refer to an absolute freedom.

5 For example, a belief that magistrates and others have always been too lenient, as Pollak suggests, promotes not only a benevolent image of the legal system but may incur an extreme authoritarian backlash. See the chapter on the treatment of female offenders for a fuller examination of this issue.

Chapter 3   Contemporary studies of female criminality

1 The argument that female emancipation will lead to an increase in crime can be found in Lombroso and Ferrero's work (1895) and probably has even earlier origins. It has been a popular theme for a considerable length of time and it appears as though it is re-emphasized at every renewal of the demand for equality for women.

2 For a critique of the XYY chromosome theory, see Taylor *et al.* (1973).

3 For example, we know that women in countries like the Soviet Union are employed in jobs like engineering and mining, which in our culture are thought to be purely masculine activities.

4 See for example, *Family Dynamics and Female Sexual Delinquency* edited by O. Pollak and A. S. Friedman (1969), *The Elegant Prostitute* by H. Greenwald (1970) and *The Psychopathology of Prostitution* by E. Glover (1969).

Chapter 4   Prostitution, rape and sexual politics

1 In some cases the existence of male prostitutes is recognized as in the implementation of the statute which makes it an offence for either men or women to live off the earnings of male or female prostitutes. However, it is only possible in the UK for a woman to be legally defined as a 'common prostitute' and the Official Statistics include only women in the category known as 'offences by prostitutes'.

2 See Susan Brownmiller's *Against our Will* (1975) for a brief historical study of the law pertaining to rape.

3 It may of course be argued that prostitution (or soliciting) should not be an offence at all. The mere fact that it is, while male clients of prostitutes remain law-abiding citizens, reflects a double-standard of morality which condemns promiscuity in women while condoning it in men. For an historical description of societal reaction to prostitution see *Prostitution and Morality* by H. Benjamin and R. Masters (1965) and 'Reflections by Gaslight' by K. A. Holmes (1972).

4 See, for example, R. Cross, *Evidence* (1967) and R. A. Hibey, 'The trial of a rape case', *American Criminal Law Review* (1973).

5 See, for example, S. Brownmiller, *Against our Will* (1975); K. Weis and S. Borges, 'Victimology and Rape' (1973); S. Griffin, 'Rape: the All-American Crime' (1971); J. and H. Schwendinger, 'Rape Myths: in Legal, Theoretical and Everyday Practice' (1974); J. M. Reynolds, 'Rape as Social Control' (1974).

6 For an analysis of the imposition of particular forms of sexual morality see W. Reich, *The Invasion of Compulsory Sex-Morality*, 1975.

7 The repression of overt sexuality depended of course on such factors as sex, age and socio-economic class. It also depended upon the context in which sexual encounters took place, for it is well known that during the Victorian era public opprobrium of sexuality co-existed with secret, private indulgences sometimes of the most extreme sort (cf. R. Pearsall, *The Worm in the Bud* (1972)). It is also likely that this type of hypocrisy was still influential at the time of Gibbens's study of juvenile prostitutes as he appears to associate female sexuality with a lack of control in the way that the Victorians did. Certainly he was writing before the so-called sexual revolution of the 1960s when it became possible to talk publicly of female sexuality, needs and desires.

8 One example of the way in which rapists are popularly portrayed as men with sexual problems or without a satisfactory sexual outlet is the case of Peter Cook, the 'Cambridge Rapist'. In newspapers such as the *Sun* and the *Daily Express* (4 October 1975) Cook was shown to be a sexual pervert who was driven to rape by watching blue films and studying pornography. It was also later revealed that his wife had refused to have sexual intercourse with him for several months and this, it was felt, played a contributory part in his becoming a rapist because it indicated that he must have been sexually frustrated.

9 The legal reinforcement of women's subordinate position and lack of rights over their own sexuality is exemplified by the law which makes it legally impossible for a man to be found guilty of the rape

of his wife. It is assumed in law that a man has free access to his wife regardless of her will.

10 Rapists are not always imprisoned and may only be fined if found guilty of rape. One example of this is the case of Patrick Moving who, after being convicted of the rapes of two women at knifepoint, was given a suspended sentence by the courts. He was then photographed by the press (i.e. the *Daily Express*, 21 June 1975) celebrating with his fiancée who still intended to marry him. In this case there would appear to be little dramatic change in the rapist's subsequent lifestyle.

11 One example of the way in which rape may become a career with a sustaining ideology and political purpose is the case of Eldridge Cleaver. In his book *Soul on Ice* (1971) he describes his career as a rapist in the following terms:

> I became a rapist. To refine my technique and *modus operandi*, I started out by practising on black girls in the ghetto ... and when I considered myself smooth enough, I crossed the tracks and sought out white prey. I did this consciously, deliberately, wilfully, methodically....
>
> Rape was an insurrectionary act. It delighted me that I was defying and trampling upon the white man's law, upon his system of values, and that I was defiling his women ... (Cleaver, 1971, p. 26).

Chapter 5   The treatment of female offenders

1 One way in which the common-law definition of rape may be said to be discriminatory is in the exclusion of wives and husbands from the law of rape. In other words, a man may not be accused of raping his wife unless they are legally separated or have been divorced. He may be accused of assault but all sexual elements of such an attack are ignored by the law. In this way the law condones potential sexual abuses of wives by husbands because the legal marriage contract assumes that the wife has given up all rights to her own body to her husband.

2 The term 'prosecutrix' is synonymous with complainant or alleged victim. It stems from the period in history when women had the burden of bringing a case against a rapist herself in order to achieve justice. Although this process is no longer necessary, because the state is empowered to take a suspected rapist to court, the term remains in legal parlance because it implies the quality of a personal prosecution. I use the term simply because in rape cases today a

substantial burden remains on the woman who has been raped, and as far as support from the police and legal services is concerned in many respects she appears to be attempting a private prosecution if she takes her case to court.

3 This is not a criticism of the sentencing policy of the courts as imprisonment or severe punishment is as unlikely to prevent the occurrence of rape as any other type of offences. However, the typical sentencing policy of the courts has some effect on the arguments which are put forward for changing the rules of evidence in rape cases. It is maintained that because rape carries a maximum sentence of life imprisonment there should be no changes made which will increase the possibility of conviction for rape. But as the maximum penalty is rarely given, and as the most usual custodial sentence is two to three years imprisonment this argument loses some of its force.

4 It is often argued as a corollary of the belief in the lenient treatment of women by the police courts and legal system that if women demand equality they must expect more severe penalties for criminal offences (cf. Smith, 1974). In view of the unproven nature of this belief in leniency such an outcome is doubtful but even were it to be shown that in some cases women are less likely to receive custodial sentences than men, an increase in severity of treatment for women is not the only possible consequence of the demand for equality. On the contrary, equality for women implies also equality for men and should the desired state of equality be achieved it is possible that the courts will take into account the kind of mitigating factors for men which they are presumed to take into account for women. For example, if a woman should not be imprisoned because she has children and because of the hardship they might suffer, similar considerations may be taken into account with a male offender given that equality would mean a greater role in childcare for many men.

5 A similar attitude towards female offenders exists in penal establishments in the USA. Margery Velimesis, in her paper on correctional programmes for women in the USA, states: 'The mediocrity and irrelevance of correctional programming for women are attributable to the misperception of the nature of women and the effects of being assigned a second-class status in society' (Velimesis, 1975, p. 105).

6 Although it is recognized that male offenders will become breadwinners and will need employment this does not automatically mean that male offenders are given the opportunities that female offenders lack. On the contrary there is a lack of appreciation about the needs for opportunities for retraining for all offenders regardless of sex.

Chapter 6   Women, crime and mental illness

1 The term 'mental illness' has been criticized by Szasz (1972) because the ideological foundations of a diagnosis of mental illness are concealed by the medical term illness. In fact he argues that such a diagnosis is predicated upon value judgment and not scientific or medical criteria. For this reason Szasz maintains that all psychiatric treatment should be voluntarily undertaken by those who are suffering and not imposed upon 'deviants' by state controlled, and ideologically oriented, institutions. While it is possible to accept this broad argument (Szasz's solution in terms of a purely private health service is however totally rejected) it must also be recognized that the term mental illness is now one that is in common currency and, in spite of the fact that it masks ideological content, the use of a different term would not remove that content. I shall therefore persist in using the concept of mental illness but in full awareness of the processes and value judgments involved in arriving at such a diagnosis.

2 The DHSS explains the diagnostic categories as follows:
Category 1 refers to all types of schizophrenia (catatonic, paranoid, latent etc.) and all types of paranoid states.
Category 2 refers to depressive psychoses, involutional melancholia, manic-depressive psychosis, manic type, depressed type, circular type and other.
Category 3 refers to anxiety neurosis, hysterical neurosis, phobic neurosis, obsessive compulsive neurosis, depressive neurosis, neurasthenia, depersonalization syndrome, hypochondriacal neurosis and other.
Category 4 includes depression not specified as neurotic or psychotic, epilepsy, undiagnosed cases and admissions for other than psychiatric disorders.

3 Special Hospitals are those which house the mentally ill who are also criminal offenders. The inmates are considered to be sufficiently dangerous to merit a more secure environment than ordinary psychiatric hospitals.

4 This contention is perhaps disputed by Professor Brown *et al.*'s (1975) study which argues that an intimate (though not necessarily sexually intimate) relationship helps to prevent breakdown. However, the fact that a couple are married does not necessarily mean there is a great deal of intimacy between them and it is possible therefore that these findings can co-exist.

Bibliography

Advisory Group on the Law of Rape (1975), *Report of the Advisory Group on the Law of Rape*, London, HMSO.

Allen, V. L. (1974), 'The common-sense guide to industrial relations', *University of Leeds Review*, vol. 17, no. 1.

Amir, M. (1967), 'Victim precipitated forcible rape', *Journal of Criminal Law, Criminology and Police Science*, vol. 58, no. 4.

Amir, M. (1971), *Patterns in Forcible Rape*, Chicago and London, University of Chicago Press.

Angrist, S. (1969), 'The study of sex roles', *Journal of Social Issues*, vol. 25, no. 1.

Ashdown-Sharp, P. (1975), *The Single Woman's Guide to Pregnancy and Parenthood*, Harmondsworth, Penguin.

Baker Miller, J. (ed.) (1974), *Psychoanalysis and Women*, Harmondsworth, Penguin.

Bebel, A. (1971), *Woman under Socialism*, New York, Schocken Books.

Benjamin, H. and Masters, R. E. L. (1965), *Prostitution and Morality*, London, Souvenir Press.

Berry, L. (1974), 'Women in society 1. A discussion on female violence', *Listener*, 7 November.

Bertrand, M. A. (1973), 'The insignificance of female criminality in the light of the hegemonic conceptions of sexual roles and the privatization of women', unpublished paper presented at the First Conference of the European Group for the Study of Deviance and Social Control, Florence.

Bishop, C. (1931), *Women and Crime*, London, Chatto & Windus.

Broverman, I. K., Broverman, D. M., Clarkson, E. E., Rosengrantz, P. S. and Vogel, S. R. (1970), 'Sex role stereotypes and clinical judgments of mental health', *Journal of Consulting and Clinical Psychology*, vol. 34, no. 1.

Brown, G., Bhrolchain, M. N. and Harris, T. (1975), 'Social class and

Bibliography

psychiatric disturbance among women in an urban population', *Sociology*, vol. 9, no. 2, May.

Brownmiller, S. (1975), *Against our Will: Men, Women and Rape*, London, Secker & Warburg.

Bryan, J. (1973), 'Apprenticeships in prostitution' and 'Occupational ideologies and individual attitudes of call girls', in E. Rubington and M. Weinberg (eds), *Deviance: the Interactionist Perspective*, 2nd edn, London, Macmillan.

Bullough, V. L. (1964), *The History of Prostitution*, New York, University Books.

Central Office of Information (1975), *Women in Britain*, Reference Pamphlet no. 67, London, HMSO.

Chesler, P. (1974), *Women and Madness*, London, Allen Lane.

Chesney-Lind, M. (1973), 'Judicial enforcement of the female sex role: the family court and the female delinquent', *Issues in Criminology*, Fall 1973, vol. 8, no. 2.

Cleaver, E. (1971), *Soul on Ice*, London, Panther.

Cohn, Y. (1970), 'Criteria for the probation officer's recommendation to the Juvenile Court Judge', in P. G. Garabedian and D. C. Gibbons (eds), *Becoming Delinquent*, Chicago, Aldine.

Connell, N. and Wilson, C. (1974), *Rape: The First Sourcebook for Women*, New York, Plume Books.

Coote, A. and Gill, T. (1975), *The Rape Controversy*, London, NCCL.

Coulter, J. (1973), *Approaches to Insanity: A Philosophical and Sociological Study*, London, Martin Robertson.

Cowie, J., Cowie, V. and Slater, E. (1968), *Delinquency in Girls*, London, Heinemann.

Cressey, D. (1971), 'Role theory, differential association and compulsive crimes', in A. M. Rose (ed.), *Human Behaviour and Social Processes*, London, Routledge & Kegan Paul.

Cross, R. (1967), *Evidence*, 3rd edn, London, Butterworth.

Dalton, K. (1961), 'Menstruation and crime', *British Medical Journal*, vol. 2, part 2, 30 December.

Davies, J. and Goodman, N. (1972), *Girl Offenders Aged 17 to 20 Years*, Home Office Research Unit Report no. 14, London, HMSO.

Davies, J., Goodman, N., Maloney, E., Durkin, P. and Halton, J. (1976), *Further Studies of Female Offenders*, Home Office Research Study no. 33, London, HMSO.

Davis, K. (1971), 'Prostitution', in R. K. Merton and R. Nisbet (eds), *Contemporary Social Problems*, 3rd edn, New York, Harcourt Brace Jovanovich.

de Beauvoir, S. (1974), *The Second Sex*, Harmondsworth, Penguin.

Dell, S. (1971), *Silent in Court*, Occasional Papers on Social Administration, no. 42, London, Bell.

Dell, S. and Gibbens, T. C. N. (1971), 'Remands of women offenders for medical reports', *Medicine, Science and the Law*, vol. 11, no. 3.

Department of Education and Science (1975), *Curricular Differences for Boys and Girls*, Educational Survey 21, London, HMSO.

d'Orban, P. T. (1971), 'Social and psychiatric aspects of female crime', *Medicine, Science and the Law*, vol. 11, no. 3.

Douglas, J. (1967), *The Social Meaning of Suicide*, Princeton. UP.

Ellis, H. (1936), *Studies in the Psychology of Sex*, vol. IV, *Prostitution*, New York, Random House.

Engels, F. (1973), *The Origin of the Family, Private Property and the State*, New York, Pathfinder Press.

Epps, P. (1962), 'Shoplifters in Holloway', in T. C. N. Gibbens and J. Prince, *Shoplifting*, London, ISTD Publication.

Eysenck, H. J. (1970), *Crime and Personality*, St Albans, Paladin.

Fairhall, J. (1976), 'The unwanted drop-out girls who take to violence', the *Guardian*, 16 January.

Faulkner, D. E. R. (1971), 'The redevelopment of Holloway Prison', *Howard Journal of Penology and Crime Prevention*, vol. 12, no. 2.

Firestone, S. (1973), *The Dialectic of Sex*, St Albans, Paladin.

Garfinkel, A., Lefcourt, C. and Schulder, D. (1971), 'Women's servitude under law', in R. Lefcourt (ed.), *Law Against the People*, New York, Vintage.

Garfinkel, H. (1967), *Studies in Ethnomethodology*, New York, Prentice-Hall.

Gelb, L. A. (1974), 'Masculinity-Femininity: a study in imposed inequality', in J. Baker Miller (ed.), *Psychoanalysis and Women*, Harmondsworth, Penguin.

Giallombardo, R. (1966), *Society of Women: A Study of a Woman's Prison*, New York, Wiley.

Giallombardo, R. (1974), *The Social World of Imprisoned Girls*, New York, Wiley.

Gibbens, T. C. N. (1957), 'Juvenile prostitution', *British Journal of Delinquency*, vol. 8.

Gibbens, T. C. N. (1971), 'Female offenders', *British Journal of Hospital Medicine*, vol. 6, September.

Gibbens, T. C. N. and Prince, J. (1962), *Shoplifting*, London, ISTD Publication.

Gibbens, T. C. N., Palmer, C. and Prince, J. (1971), 'Mental health aspects of shoplifting', *British Medical Journal*, vol. 3, 11 September.

Gilley, J. (1974), 'How to help the raped', *New Society*, vol. 28, no. 612.

Bibliography

Glover, E. (1969), *The Psychopathology of Prostitution*, London, ISTD Publication.

Glueck, S. and Glueck, G. (1934), *Five Hundred Delinquent Women*, New York, Knopf.

Goldman, E. (1970), *The Traffic in Women and Other Essays on Feminism*, Washington, Times Change Press.

Goodman, N. and Price, J. (1967), *Studies of Female Offenders*, Home Office Research Unit Report no. 11, London, HMSO.

Gove, W. R. (1972), 'The relationship between sex roles, marital status and mental illness', *Social Forces*, vol. 51, no. 1.

Gove, W. R. and Tudor, J. F. (1973), 'Adult sex roles and mental illness', *American Journal of Sociology*, vol. 78, no. 4.

Greenwald, H. (1958), *The Call Girl*, New York, Ballantine Books.

Greenwald, H. (1970), *The Elegant Prostitute*, New York, Walker & Company.

Greer, G. (1970), *The Female Eunuch*, St Albans, Paladin.

Griffin, S. (1971), 'Rape: the all-American crime', *Ramparts*, September.

Hall-Williams, J. E. (1970), *The English Penal System in Transition*, London, Butterworth.

Halsbury's Statutes of England (1969), 3rd edn, vol. 8, London, Butterworth.

Hart, T. (1975), 'The new adolescent offender', unpublished paper presented at the Institute for the Study and Treatment of Delinquency Spring Conference, 1975.

Heffernan, E. (1972), *Making it in Prison*, New York, Wiley.

Heidensohn, F. (1968), 'The deviance of women: a critique and an enquiry', *British Journal of Sociology*, vol. 19, no. 2.

Heidensohn, F. (1970), 'Sex, crime and society', in G. A. Harrison and J. Perl (eds), *Biosocial Aspects of Sex*, Oxford and Edinburgh, Blackwell.

Henriques, F. (1968), *Modern Sexuality*, vol. III *Prostitution and Society*, London, MacGibbon & Kee.

Herschberger, R. (1970), *Adam's Rib*, New York, Harper & Row.

Hibey, R. A. (1973), 'The trial of a rape case', *American Criminal Law Review*, vol. 2, part 2.

Hindess, B. (1973), *The Use of Official Statistics in Sociology: a critique of Positivism and Ethnomethodology*, London, Macmillan.

Hoffman-Bustamante, D. (1973), 'The nature of female criminality', *Issues in Criminology*, vol. 8, no. 2.

Holmes, Kay A. (1972), 'Reflections by gaslight: prostitution in another age', *Issues in Criminology*, vol. 7, no. 1.

Holmstrom, L. L. and Burgess, A. W. (1975), 'Rape: the victim and the criminal justice system', *International Journal of Criminology and Penology*, vol. 3, no. 2.

Horney, K. (1974) 'The problem of feminine masochism', in J. Baker Miller (ed.), *Psychoanalysis and Women*, Harmondsworth, Penguin.

Kinsey, A. C., Pomeroy, W. B. and Martin, C. E. (1963), *Sexual Behaviour in the Human Male*, Philadelphia and London, W. B. Saunders.

Klein, D. (1973), 'The etiology of female crime: a review of the literature', *Issues in Criminology*, vol. 8, no. 2.

Koller, K. M. (1971), 'Parental deprivation, family background and female delinquency', *British Journal of Psychiatry*, vol. 118, pp. 319–27.

Konopka, G. (1966), *The Adolescent Girl in Conflict*, New Jersey, Prentice-Hall.

Laing, R. D. and Esterson, A. (1970), *Sanity, Madness and the Family*, Harmondsworth, Penguin.

Lemert, E. (1967), *Human Deviance, Social Problems and Social Control*, New York, Prentice-Hall.

Linn, E. (1961), 'Agents, timing and events leading to mental hospitalization', *Human Organization*, vol. 20, no. 2, Summer.

Lombroso, C. and Ferrero, W. (1895), *The Female Offender*, London, Fisher Unwin.

Macdonald, J. M. (1975), *Rape: Offenders and their Victims*, Illinois, Charles C. Thomas.

Mackenzie, M. (1975), *Shoulder to Shoulder*, Harmondsworth, Penguin.

McRobbie, A. and Garber, J. (1975), 'Girls and subcultures: an exploration', *Working Papers in Cultural Studies*, vols 7 and 8, University of Birmingham, Centre for Contemporary Cultural Studies.

Mannheim, H. (1965), *Comparative Criminology*, London, Routledge & Kegan Paul.

Matza, D. (1969), *Becoming Deviant*, New York, Prentice-Hall.

Mead, M. (1967), *Male and Female*, Harmondsworth, Penguin.

Miller, W. B. (1973), 'The Molls', *Society*, vol. 11, no. 1.

Millman, M. (1975) 'She did it all for love: a feminist view of the sociology of deviance', in M. Millman and R. Moss Kanter (eds), *Another Voice: Feminist Perspectives on Social Life and Social Science*, New York, Anchor Books.

Mitchell, J. (1974), *Psychoanalysis and Feminism*, London, Allen Lane.

Morris, R. (1964), 'Female delinquency and relational problems', *Social Forces*, vol. 43, no. 1.

Morris, R. (1965), 'Attitudes towards Delinquency by Delinquents, Non-Delinquents and their friends', *British Journal of Criminology*, vol. 5.

Mulvihill, D., Tumin, M. and Curtis, L. (1969), *Crimes of Violence*, vol. 12, Washington, USA, Government Printing Office.

Oakley, A. (1972), *Sex, Gender and Society*, London, Temple Smith.

Bibliography

Oakley, A. (1974), *The Sociology of Housework*, London, Martin Robertson.
Pearsall, R. (1972), *The Worm in the Bud*, Harmondsworth, Penguin.
Pearson, G. (1975), *The Deviant Imagination*, London, Macmillan.
Phillips, D. L. and Segal, B. E. (1969), 'Sexual Status and Psychiatric Symptoms', *American Sociological Review*, vol. 34, no. 1.
Platt, A. (1969), *The Child Savers*, London, University of Chicago Press.
Pollak, O. (1961), *The Criminality of Women*, New York, A. S. Barnes.
Pollak, O. and Friedman, A. S. (eds) (1969), *Family Dynamics and Female Sexual Delinquency*, California, Science & Behaviour Books.
Pratt, P. (1974), 'Why women turn to crime', *Observer*, 8 December.
Radical Alternatives to Prison (1974), *Alternatives to Holloway*, London, RAP.
Radzinowicz, L. (1937), 'Variability of the sex-ratio of criminality', *Sociological Review*, vol. 29.
Reich, W. (1975), *The Invasion of Compulsory Sex Morality*, Harmondsworth, Penguin.
Reynolds, J. M. (1974), 'Rape as social control', *Catalyst*, no. 8, Winter.
Richardson, H. (1969), *Adolescent Girls in Approved Schools*, London, Routledge & Kegan Paul.
Rolph, C. H. (1955), *Women of the Streets*, London, Secker & Warburg.
Rosenblum, K. E. (1975), 'Female deviance and the female sex role: a preliminary investigation', *British Journal of Sociology*, vol. 26, no. 2.
Rushing, W. (1971), 'Individual resources, societal reaction, and hospital commitment', *American Journal of Sociology*, vol. 77, no. 3, November.
Scheff, T. (1974), 'The labelling theory of mental illness', *American Sociological Review*, vol. 39, June.
Schofield, M. (1975), 'A new prescription for the pill', *New Society*, vol. 34, no. 683.
Schwendinger, J. and H. (1974), 'Rape myths: in legal, theoretical and everyday practice', *Crime and Social Justice*, vol. 1, no. 1.
Select Committee on Violence in Marriage (1975), *Report from the Select Committee on Violence in Marriage*, vol. 1, session 1974–75, London, HMSO.
Sexual Offences (Amendment) Bill (1975), London, HMSO.
Shoham, S. G. (1974), *Society and the Absurd*, Oxford, Blackwell.
Smith, A. (1962), *Women in Prison*, London, Stevens.
Smith, A. (1974), 'The woman offender', in L. Blom-Cooper (ed.), *Progress in Penal Reform*, Oxford, Clarendon Press.
Smith, D. (1973), 'Women's perspective as a radical critique of sociology', *Sociological Inquiry*, vol. 44, no. 1.
Smith, L. Shacklady (1975), 'Female delinquency and social reaction',

unpublished paper presented at the University of Essex, Women and Deviancy Conference, Spring 1975.

Smith, J. C. and Hogan, B. (1973), *Criminal Law*, London, Butterworth.

Sutherland, E. H. and Cressey, D. (1966), *Principles of Criminology*, Philadelphia, J. P. Lippincott.

Suval, E. M. and Brisson, R. C. (1974), 'Neither beauty nor beast: female criminal homicide offenders', *International Journal of Criminology and Penology*, vol. 2, no. 1.

Szasz, T. (1972), *The Myth of Mental Illness*, St Albans, Paladin.

Taylor, I., Walton, P. and Young, J. (1973), *The New Criminology*, London, Routledge & Kegan Paul.

Taylor, I., Walton, P. and Young, J. (1975), *Critical Criminology*, London, Routledge & Kegan Paul.

Taylor, L. and Cohen, S. (1972), *Psychological Survival*, Harmondsworth, Penguin.

Terry, R. M. (1970), 'Discrimination in the handling of juvenile offenders by social control agencies', in P. G. Garabedian and D. C. Gibbons (eds), *Becoming Delinquent*, Chicago, Aldine Press.

Thomas, W. I. (1907), *Sex and Society*, Boston, Little Brown.

Thomas, W. I. (1967), *The Unadjusted Girl*, New York, Harper & Row.

Thompson, C. (1974), 'Some effects of the derogatory attitude toward female sexuality', in J. Baker Miller (ed.), *Psychoanalysis and Women*, Harmondsworth, Penguin.

Vedder, C. B. and Sommerville, D. B. (1970), *The Delinquent Girl*, Illinois, Charles C. Thomas.

Velimesis, M. (1975), 'The female offender', *Crime and Delinquency Literature*, vol. 7, no. 1.

Walker, N. (1973), *Crime and Punishment in Britain*, University of Edinburgh Press.

Ward, D. A. and Kassebaum, G. G. (1966), *Women's Prison*, London, Weidenfeld & Nicolson.

Ward, D. A., Jackson, M. and Ward, R. (1969), 'Crimes of violence by women', in D. Mulvihill *et al.* (eds), *Crimes of Violence*, vol. 13, Washington, US Government Printing Office.

Weis, K. and Borges, S. (1973), 'Victimology and rape: the case of the legitimate victim', *Issues in Criminology*, vol. 8, no. 2.

Weisstein, N. (1971), 'Psychology constructs the female', in V. Gornick and B. K. Moran (eds), *Woman in Sexist Society*, New York, Basic Books.

Wiles, P. N. P. (1970), 'Criminal statistics and sociological explanations of crime', in P. N. P. Wiles and W. G. Carson (eds), *Crime and Delinquency in Britain*, London, Martin Robertson.

Bibliography

Wilson, C. (1974), 'Dominance and sex', in L. Gross (ed.), *Sexual Behaviour*, London and New York, Wiley.

Winn, D. (1974), *Prostitutes*, London, Hutchinson.

Wise, N. (1967), 'Juvenile delinquency among middle class girls', in E. Vaz (ed.), *Middle Class Juvenile Delinquency*, New York, Harper & Row.

Wolfenden, J. (1957), *Report of the Committee on Homosexual Offences and Prostitution* (Cmnd 247), London, HMSO.

Wolfgang, M. E. (1958), *Patterns in Criminal Homicide*, University of Pennsylvania Press.

Working Party on Vagrancy and Street Offences (1974), *Working Party on Vagrancy and Street Offences Working Paper*, London, HMSO.

Wright Mills, C. (1943), 'The professional ideology of social pathologists', *American Journal of Sociology*, vol. 49, no. 2.

Name index

Subject index

Subject index

Sexual abnormality, 33–5, 58, 94

Sexual bargaining, 44, 102–3

Sexual craving, 80

Sexual division of labour, 90

Sexual exploitation, 90–1, 93, 104–5, 107

Sexual Offences Act 1967, 6

Sexual Offences (Amendment) Bill, 126f.

Sexual promiscuity, 11–13, 20f., 38, 44, 81, 84, 132f.

Shoplifting, 5, 8f., 24, 110–11, 184

'Sickness' analogy, 149

Social control, 4, 27, 29, 41–2, 61

Social work organizations, 37, 45, 61, 184

Socialization, 66, 68, 100–1, 172; 'poor' socialization, 69

Societal reaction, 69, 72–3, 155

Soliciting, 77; *see also* Prostitution

Special hospitals, 165–6, 196

Street Offences Act 1959, 113, 115, 116, 191

Subcultural theory, 183

Treatment, 43, 61, 108f., 144, 148, 184

Uni-sex, 71

Victim precipitation, 99f., 180

Violence, xii, 2, 16, 72, 96

Wolfenden Committee, 113f., 191

Women: criminal law and, 112f.; criminal process and, 128f.; inferior status of, xi, 26, 35, 38, 49, 65, 69, 76, 107, 141, 185; invisibility of, 1, 178, 180f.; mental breakdown and, 2, 146f.; oppression of, 45, 182; penal system and, 140f.; primitive nature of, 32, 79–80; as subject of study, 178f.; symbolic value of, 43; 'true' nature of, 30, 35, 58–9, 111

Women's Movement and crime, 24–6, 54, 70–6, 182, 192

Working Party on Vagrancy and Street Offences, 115f.

XYY chromosome theory, 57, 192